Wit Hits The Spot

Humorous quotation books from Prion

Des MacHale
Wit
Wit on Target
(previously entitled *Yet More Wit*)
Wit Rides Again
Wit — The Last Laugh

Aubrey Dillon Malone
The Cynic's Dictionary

Stephen Robins
The Importance of Being Idle
How to be a Complete Dandy
The Ruling Asses — a little book of political stupidity

Michelle Lovric
Women's Wicked Wit

Rosemary Jarski
Wisecracks — Great lines from the Hollywood movies
Hollywood Wit — Classic off-screen quips and quotes

Wit Hits The Spot

Des MacHale

PRION

This book is dedicated to Patricia and Kieran with much love

This edition published in 2001 by
Prion Books Ltd.,
Imperial Works, Perren Street,
London NW5 3ED

First published 1997 entitled More Wit

Copyright © Des MacHale 1997

A catalogue record of this book can be obtained
from the British Library

ISBN 1-85375-468-4

Printed and bound in Great Britain by
Bookmarque, Croydon, Surrey

Contents

Introduction

WHEN I compiled my first book of humorous quotations, I rashly claimed that it was the best such collection ever assembled. I believed this so strongly that I offered to eat without seasoning any better and funnier collection provided by anyone. Well I wonder what boiled book without salt tastes like because the current collection of witty quotes is as good if not better than my previous effort. I am astonished that so many genuinely funny quotes remain, but then humour and wit are like seams of gold that never run out.

Previously, I've stuck my neck out by naming my choice of over thirty of the greatest wits of all time, led by Oscar Wilde, Woody Allen and Mark Twain, and, to my surprise, my list met with widespread approval. There was not a single dissenting voice to any of my choices, but in putting together my current anthology, I began to realise that many other newer wits could be added to the roll of honour. My favourites at the moment would include Dave Barry, A. A. Gill, Jo Brand, Dan Quayle (unwittingly!) and Roy Brown.

Since my day job involves being a mathematician (please don't hold that against me, ATBSTTA) I am very interested in ordering, classifying and grading. I would very much like to list the World's Wittiest Quotes, a hundred of the best and if readers would like to nominate their choices, say ten per person, I will certainly take their opinions into account in making my final choice.

As always, this collection of over two thousand witty quotes is meant to be enjoyed by speakers, teachers, even comedians, to liven up their material. Separate copies should be kept by the bedside, in all loos and at the dinner table so that no opportunity is missed to convulse others and bask in the reflected glory of the world's greatest wits. Dear reader, I envy you, because I have now read all these quotes many times but you are about to dip into many of them for the first time. Enjoy!

Des MacHale
Cork

Art

The English public takes no interest in a work of art until it is told that the work in question is immoral.

Oscar Wilde

The reason that some portraits don't look true to life is that some people make no effort to resemble their pictures.

Salvador Dali

You stay here for a moment. I'll go upstairs and fetch the etchings.

James Thurber

The Venus de Milo is a good example of what happens to somebody who won't stop biting her fingernails.

Will Rogers

All my life I have wanted to be a great painter in oils. I am tired of politics and as soon as I have carried out my programme in Germany, I shall take up my painting. I feel that I have it in myself to become one of the great artists of the age and that future historians will remember me, not for what I have done for Germany, but for my art.

Adolf Hitler

Every morning when I awake, I experience a supreme pleasure – that of being Salvador Dali

Salvador Dali

Right now I'm the greatest. I don't say this out of vanity – it's just that the rest are so bad.

Salvador Dali

The enemy of all painting is the colour grey.

Delacroix

When I had to fill in a census paper, I gave my profession as genius and my infirmity as talent.

Oscar Wilde

It's God – I recognised him from Blake's picture.

Robert Frost

If more than ten per cent of the population likes a painting, it should be burned, for it must be bad.

George Bernard Shaw

I've posed nude for a photographer in the manner of Rodin's Thinker, but I looked merely constipated.

George Bernard Shaw

I don't own any of my own paintings because a Picasso original costs several thousand dollars and that's a luxury I cannot afford.

Pablo Picasso

Immature artists imitate, mature artists steal.

Lionel Trilling

I believe I am the only Irishman apart from the staff who has ever set foot in the National Gallery of Ireland.

George Bernard Shaw

If it were not for the intellectual snobs who pay in solid cash, the arts would perish with their starving practitioners.

Aldous Huxley

The murals in restaurants are about on a par with the food in art galleries.

Peter DeVries

Art

Edith Sitwell's interest in art was largely confined to portraits of herself.

John Fowles

Business and Money

The poor shall inherit the earth, but not its mineral rights.
J. Paul Getty

If it's a bill, the Post Office will get it to you in twenty-four hours, if it's a cheque, allow them a couple of weeks.
Richard Needham

Blessed are the young, for they shall inherit the national debt.
Herbert Hoover

As the economy gets better, everything else gets worse.
Art Buchwald

I don't want money. It is only people who pay their bills who want money and I never pay mine.
Oscar Wilde

Nothing dispels enthusiasm like a small admission fee.
Kin Hubbard

The hardest thing in the world to understand is income tax.
Albert Einstein

If economists were any good at business, they would be rich men instead of advisors to rich men.
Kirk Kerkorian

I was never very good at mathematics, but I do understand numbers with a bunch of zeros at the end.
Chi Chi Rodriguez

Rich people cannot understand poverty. They find it very hard to understand why people who want dinner do not just ring the bell.
Walter Bagehot

Business and Money

I have never heard two Americans talking without the word dollar being spoken between them.

Frances Trollope

You can generally tell whether a man is an economist by the number of times he uses the phrase: "All other things being equal."

William Davis

Simple rules for saving money: to save half, when you are fired by an eager impulse to contribute to a charity, wait and count forty. To save three-quarters, count sixty. To save it all, count seventy-five.

Mark Twain

If someone says "It's not the money, it's the principle", it's the money.

Angelo Valenti

If Max Beaverbrook ever gets to heaven, he won't last long. He will be chucked out for trying to pull off a merger between heaven and hell – after having secured a controlling interest in key subsidiary companies in both places of course.

H. G. Wells

The man who writes the bank's advertising slogan is not the same man who makes the loans.

George Coote

One difference between death and taxes is that death doesn't get worse every time Congress meets.

Roy L. Schaefer

A habit of debt is very injurious to the memory.

Austin O'Malley

I wouldn't trust a bank that would lend money to such a poor risk as me.

Robert Benchley

Most people favour an incomes policy – provided it doesn't apply to them.

Frank Cousins

The quickest way to get rid of people is to lend them money.

Anita Blackmon

Did you know that bills travel through the post at five times the speed of cheques?

Charles Dollen

If something's old and you're trying to sell it, it's obsolete; if you're trying to buy it, it's a collector's item.

Frank Ross

Never buy a portable television set in the street from a man who is out of breath.

Arnold Glasow

I gave Allen an unlimited budget and he exceeded it.

Edward Williams

A study of economics usually reveals that the best time to buy anything was last year.

Marty Allen

It is difficult to love mankind unless one has a reasonable private income and when one has a reasonable private income one has better things to do than to love mankind.

Hugh Kingsmill

Why should we women mind if men have their faces on the money as long as we have our hands on it?

Ivy Priest

Business and Money

There is a certain Buddhistic calm that comes from having money in the bank.

Tom Robbins

The poor will inherit the earth but the rich will inherit the church.

James A. Pike

Rich widows are the only second-hand goods that sell for first-class prices.

Benjamin Franklin

Ninety per cent of my money I spend on women and whiskey. The rest I just waste.

Tug McGraw

A statistician is someone who is good at figures but who doesn't have the personality to be an accountant.

Roy Hyde

If at first you don't succeed – you're fired.

Jean Graman

If you think nobody cares whether you are alive or dead, try missing a couple of car payments.

Ann Landers

I can speak with authority on the subject of being hard up. I have been a provincial actor.

Jerome K. Jerome

Millionaires are marrying their secretaries because they are so busy making money they haven't time to see other girls.

Doris Lilly

Only the little people pay taxes.

Leona Helmsley

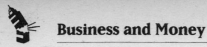

An amateur is one who plays games for the love of the thing. Unlike the professional, he receives no salary, and is contented with presents of clothes, clubs, rackets, cigarettes, cups, cheques, hotel expenses, fares and so on.

J. B. Morton

He was so crooked that when he died, they had to screw him into the ground.

Bob Hope

My office hours are twelve to one with an hour off for lunch.

George S. Kaufman

Jeffrey Bernard once tried to pay the rent by "borrowing" half a crown from twenty-four people in Soho every Friday night in the hope that they were drunk enough to have forgotten the loan by the next Friday.

Graham Lord

Elbert Gary of the United Steel Company never saw a blast furnace until after he was dead.

Benjamin Stolberg

Lots of folk confuse destiny with bad management.

Kin Hubbard

Bing Crosby doesn't pay income tax any more. He just asks the government how much they need.

Bob Hope

My consciousness is fine; it's my pay that needs raising.

Phyllis Diller

Aside from its purchasing power, money is useless as far as I'm concerned.

Alfred Hitchcock

Business and Money

How come it's a penny for your thoughts but you have to put your two cents' worth in? Somebody's making a penny.

Steven Wright

There is no petting -- modern couples just strip their clothes off and go at it. Blame must be placed on ex-President Nixon's decision to let the US dollar float in relation to other Western currencies. More than a decade of monetary instability has conditioned people to utilise their assets immediately. If the sex urge is not spent forthwith, it might degenerate into something less valuable – affection, for instance.

P. J. O'Rourke

I am a sensitive writer, actor, director. Talking business disgusts me. If you want to talk business, call my disgusting personal manager.

Sylvester Stallone

In college, Yuppies major in business administration. If to meet certain requirements they have to take a liberal arts course, they take Business Poetry.

Dave Barry

Recession is when the woman next door loses her job. Slump is when the woman in your house loses her job. Recovery is when the woman in No. 10 loses hers.

Len Murray

Women prefer men who have something tender about them – especially the legal kind.

Kay Ingram

Today it takes more brains and effort to make out the income tax form than it does to make the income.

Alfred E. Neumann

Business and Money

The difference between the crash of 1929 and present day stock market crashes is that nowadays computers are jumping out of the windows.

Stanley Morgan

Next to being shot at and missed, nothing is really quite as satisfying as an income tax refund.

F. J. Raymond

Under capitalism man exploits man. Under communism it's just the opposite.

J. K. Galbraith

It's not many comedians today can demand a four figure fee like me — eleven pounds seventy-five pence.

Roy Brown

I'm tired of Love: I'm still more tired of Rhyme. But Money gives me pleasure all the time.

Hilaire Belloc

Nature has no cure for the madness of Bolshevism, though I have known a legacy from a rich relative to work wonders.

F. E. Smith

The only tough stitch on a pair of trousers is the stitch that affixes the price tag.

Larry Bryant

Money isn't everything, but it sure keeps you in touch with your children.

J. Paul Getty

I wanted to buy some carpeting – do you know what they wanted for carpeting? $15 a square yard. I am not going to pay that for carpeting. So what I did, I bought two square yards and when I go home I strap them to my feet.

Steve Martin

I lent a friend of mine ten thousand dollars for plastic surgery and now I don't know what he looks like.

Emo Philips

My boss has a brain like Einstein's – dead since 1955.

Gene Perret

Economics is the only field in which two people can share a Nobel Prize for saying opposing things.

Roberto Alazar

There is no such thing as a free lunch.

Milton Friedman

Early to bed and early to rise probably indicates unskilled labour.

John Ciardi

Gold-tipped cigarettes are awfully expensive; I can afford them only when I am in debt.

Oscar Wilde

Duty *n*. That which sternly impels us in the direction of profit, along the lines of desire.

Ambrose Bierce

Then the insurance man told me that the accident policy covered falling off the roof but not hitting the ground.

Tommy Cooper

Business and Money

If you put two economists in a room, you get two opinions, unless one of them is Keynes, in which case you get three opinions.

Winston Churchill

If you don't believe in the resurrection of the dead, look at any office at quitting time.

Robert Townsend

Nowadays a citizen can hardly distinguish between a tax and a fine, except that the fine is generally much lighter.

G. K. Chesterton

A money order would have saved the prodigal son the trouble of coming home.

Arthur Baer

Gentility is what is left over from rich ancestors after the money is gone.

John Ciardi

Balancing the budget is like going to heaven. Everybody wants to do it but nobody wants to make the trip.

Phil Gramm

A fool and his money are some party.

James Van Der Bosch

I haven't read Karl Marx – I got stuck on that footnote on page two.

Harold Wilson

Rich bachelors should be taxed. It is not fair that some men should be happier than others.

Oscar Wilde

I wish the banks would just say, "Look you ****, line up there, we don't give a **** about your miserable little bank account."

Paul Fussell

Nobody ever went broke saving money.

Mark Twain

He had sixty-three ways of getting money, the most common and most honourable being stealing, thieving and robbing.

François Rabelais

The rich aren't like us – they pay less taxes.

Peter DeVries

In this world, nothing is certain but death and taxes.

Benjamin Franklin

I used to feel I was being followed and watched all the time but now I pay cash for everything.

Bob Hope

Don't gamble: buy some good stock, hold it until it goes up and then sell it – if it doesn't go up, don't buy it!

Will Rogers

Money cannot buy health but I'd settle for a diamond studded wheelchair.

Dorothy Parker

He's so tight that if you stuck a piece of coal up his ass, in two weeks you'd have a diamond.

Matthew Broderick

Business conventions are important because they demonstrate how many people a company can operate without.

J. K. Galbraith

Never steal a doormat: if you do you'll be arrested, hanged and maybe reformed; steal a bank.

Finley Peter Dunne

The salary of the chief executive of a large corporation is not a market award for achievement. It is frequently a warm personal gesture by the individual to himself.

J. K. Galbraith

Please Lord, let me prove to you that winning the lottery won't spoil me.

Victoria Wood

Make money and the whole nation will conspire to call you a gentleman.

George Bernard Shaw

Never steal more than you actually need, for the possession of money leads to extravagance, foppish attitude and frivolous thought.

Dalton Trumbo

Looking at Clinton's economic program, I feel like a mosquito in a nudist colony. The real question is where to strike first.

Phil Gramm

A dollar saved is a quarter earned.

John Ciardi

Drink and other Drugs

Drink and other Drugs

What I cannot understand about Castlemaine XXXX is how they get the cat to squat over the can.

Glenn Lazarus

I have overcome my will-power and have taken up smoking again.

Mark Twain

I prefer temperance hotels – although they sell worse liquor than any other kind of hotel.

Artemus Ward

I have never led the tour in money winnings, but I have many times in alcohol consumption.

Fuzzy Zoeller

It was my Uncle George who discovered that alcohol was a food, well in advance of modern medical thought.

P. G. Wodehouse

I'm attending Alcoholics Anonymous, but it's difficult to remain anonymous.

George Best

For the past seventeen years I have been experimenting with lager. I am a lager user and one drug leads to another. If you do lager, as night follows day, you'll end up doing Kentucky Fried Chicken.

Ben Elton

I'd stay away from Ecstasy. This is a drug so strong it makes white people think they can dance.

Lenny Henry

God was an alcoholic. He created the world when he woke up with a hangover.

Peter Cook

I can tell I've had enough to drink when my knees start to bend backwards.

W. C. Fields

Even though a number of people have tried, no one has yet found a way to drink for a living.

Jean Kerr

Alcohol is an admirable commodity which enables parliament to do things at eleven at night that no sane person would do at eleven in the morning.

George Bernard Shaw

I'm off for a quiet pint – followed by fifteen noisy ones.

Gareth Chilcott

Drugs have taught an entire generation of kids the metric system.

P. J. O'Rourke

I drink champagne when I am happy and when I'm sad. Sometimes I drink it when I'm alone. When I have company I consider it obligatory. I trifle with it if I'm not hungry and drink it when I am. Otherwise I never touch it – unless I'm thirsty.

Lily Bollinger

Boozing does not necessarily have to go hand in hand with being a writer, as seems to be the concept in America. I therefore solemnly declare to all young men trying to become writers that they do not actually have to become drunkards first.

Nelson Aldrich

Drink and other Drugs

The only Irish known to R. M. Smyllie was whiskey, which he drank from a hand covered in a white glove, a consequence of a promise to his mother on her death-bed that he would "never touch a drop again".

Declan Kiberd

I saw a notice which said "Drink Canada Dry" so I've started.

Brendan Behan

Doctors don't ask the right questions to find out whether you have a drink problem. They should ask things like, "Have you ever woken up on a plane to Turkey? Has Oliver Reed ever said to you 'Push off, mate, I'm going home now.'?" That's a drink problem.

Jenny Lecoat

Now they're calling drugs an epidemic – that's 'cos white folks are doing them.

Richard Pryor

Drown in a vat of whiskey? Death where is thy sting?

W. C. Fields

The Swiss Tavern in Soho is the only pub in England that has no mice behind the snack bar. The rats have killed them all.

Jeffrey Bernard

When I was a baby being wheeled out in my pram people used to think I was deformed. I was just drunk.

Brendan Behan

I am a teetotaller because my family has already paid its debt to the distilling industry so munificently as to leave me no further obligation.

George Bernard Shaw

Drink and other Drugs

I am a strict teetotaller, not taking anything between drinks.

James Joyce

I hate people taking drugs and not giving any to me.

Alexei Sayle

I had a bad cold and a fellow told me that the best thing to do for it was to drink a quart of whiskey and go home to bed. On the way home another fellow told me the same thing. That made a half gallon.

Mark Twain

Beauty is in the eye of the beerholder.

W. C. Fields

Drink is your enemy – love your enemies.

W. C. Fields

My illness is due to my doctor's insistence that I drink milk, a whitish fluid they force down helpless babies.

W. C. Fields

I chain smoke cigarettes, but my hands shake so much I need help to light them.

Oscar Levant

I never drink water – I'm afraid it will become habit forming.

W. C. Fields

If you can stay in love for more than two years, you're on something.

Fran Lebowitz

He was to the bottle what Louis Armstrong was to the trumpet.

Jaffrey Saeed

Drink and other Drugs

I'll be sober tomorrow, but you'll be crazy for the rest of your life.

W. C. Fields

I envy people who drink – at least they know what to blame everything on.

Oscar Levant

I said to the officer who arrested me for drunk driving, "drunk definitely, but I don't know if you could call it driving".

Rob Lowe

It has always been my rule never to smoke when asleep and never to refrain when awake.

Mark Twain

I never drink water – look at the way it rusts pipes.

W. C. Fields

Education

What's the matter, do you think my fallacy is wrong?

Marshall McLuhan

The purpose of a Downside education is to prepare one for death.

Auberon Waugh

Candidates should not attempt more than six of the Ten Commandments.

Robert Benchley

The last humiliation of an aged scholar is when his juniors conspire to print a volume of essays and offer it to him as a sign that they now consider him senile.

Robin Collingwood

I am about to, or I am going to, die – both expressions are used.

Dominique Bouhours

When I was a boy the classroom had icicles inside every window at this time of year. We were savagely beaten three times a week and made to run half-naked in the snow. But the toughest NUPE mass-murderer starts blubbing if you suggest that one little kiddie might have to queue a little longer for its din-dins.

Auberon Waugh

I can't understand all the fuss about student grants. Carol managed to save out of hers. Of course we paid for her skiing holidays.

Margaret Thatcher

Education

Any student will tell you that the longest five minutes in the world are the last five minutes of a lecture, while the shortest five minutes are the last five minutes of an exam.

Karl Newell

We schoolmasters must temper discretion with deceit.

Evelyn Waugh

The advantage of a classical education is that it enables you to despise the wealth which it prevents you from achieving.

Russell Green

Professors must have a theory as a dog must have fleas.

William J. Bryan

When I was a student at the Sorbonne in Paris I used to go out and riot occasionally. I can't remember now whose side it was on.

John Foster Dulles

If any institution is controlled and led by Etonians all will be well.

Lord Plummer

There's a curious sort of statute of limitations in the learned world which makes it impossible to call a man a liar if he has gone on lying successfully for fifty years.

Ronald A. Knox

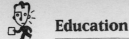

History does not repeat itself; historians merely repeat each other.

Philip Guedalla

Before I came here I was confused about this subject. Having listened to your lecture, I am still confused. But on a higher level.

Enrico Fermi

Children who have difficulty with "cat" or "car" have no difficulty with four letter words.

Pam Brown

It is regrettable that, among the Rights of Man, the right of contradicting oneself has been forgotten.

Baudelaire

In England, at any rate, education produces no effect whatsoever. If it did, it would prove a serious danger to the upper classes, and would probably lead to acts of violence in Grosvenor Square.

Oscar Wilde

Nicholas Udall, the Headmaster of Eton, stole the college plate, was homosexual, went to jail and on coming out was made Headmaster of Westminster. Those were the days.

George Lyttleton

It used to take me all vacation to grow a new hide in place of the one they flogged off me during school term.

Mark Twain

At high school, I took a little English, a little math, some science, some hubcaps and some wheel covers.

Gates Brown

My grades were four F's and a D. My tutor suggested I was spending too much time on one subject.

Shelby Metcalf

The dawn of legibility in his handwriting has revealed his utter inability to spell.

Ian Hay

Give a student from the University of Chicago a glass of water and he says: "This is a glass of water. But is it a glass of water? And if it is a glass of water, why is it a glass of water?" And eventually he dies of thirst.

Shelley Berman

He had a degree so he could ice cakes with joined-up writing.

A. A. Gill

There aren't many left like him nowadays, what with education and whiskey the price it is.

Evelyn Waugh

Lack of education is an extraordinary handicap when one is being offensive.

Josephine Tey

Education

My plan is as cunning as the fox who was Professor of
Cunning at the University of Oxford.

Rowan Atkinson

A gentleman need not know Latin; but at least he should
have forgotten it.

Brander Matthews

Our principal writers have nearly all been fortunate in
escaping education.

Hugh MacDiarmid

University politics make me long for the simplicity of the
Middle East.

Henry Kissinger

Why doesn't somebody set up an organisation for the
children of gifted parents?

Patrick Murray

Why is this thus? What is the reason of this thusness?

Artemus Ward

A good education is the next best thing to a pushy mother.

Charles Schulz

The original Greek is of great use in elucidating Browning's
translation of Agamemnon.

Robert Tyrrell

I never graduated from Iowa. I was there for only two terms – Truman's and Eisenhower's.

Alex Karras

We are going to have the best educated American people in the world.

Dan Quayle

The dumber people think you are, the more surprised they are going to be when you kill them.

William Clayton

University politics are vicious precisely because the stakes are so small.

Henry Kissinger

There is many a best-seller that could have been prevented by a good teacher.

Flannery O'Connor

He was so thick he couldn't tell which way a lift was going if he got two guesses.

Roy Brown

When I went to college, my parents threw a going away party for me, according to the letter.

Emo Philips

In any election, the candidate supported by the teachers' union is always the one to vote against.

Max Rafferty

There is no crisis to which academics will not respond with a conference.

Marvin Bressler

The only people who learn from computer-assisted instruction are the authors of the software.

Ben Schneiderman

The University has turned out many fine young men – it turned out me too.

Josh Billings

No one has ever passed so few examinations as I have and received so many degrees.

Winston Churchill

Many things do not happen as they ought. Most things do not happen at all. It is for the conscientious historian to correct these defects.

Herodotus

Foolproof systems do not take into account the ingenuity of fools.

Gene Brown

The juvenile sea squirt wanders through the ocean searching for a suitable rock or hunk of coral to cling to and make its home for life. When it finds its spot and takes root, it doesn't need its brain anymore, so it eats it. It's rather like getting tenure.

Michael Scriven

Old MacDonald was dyslexic, IEIEO.

Billy Connolly

My dog ate my homework, teacher. It's true. I had to force him, but he did eat it.

Jimmy Edwards

Hegel set out his philosophy with so much obscurity that people thought it must be profound.

Bertrand Russell

Philosophers before Kant had a tremendous advantage over philosophers after Kant in that they didn't have to waste years studying Kant.

Bertrand Russell

I have known two professors of Greek who ceased speaking to one another because of divergent views on the pluperfect subjunctive.

Stephen Leacock

If there were a verb meaning "to believe falsely", it would not have any significant first person, present indicative.

Ludwig Wittgenstein

Education

America believes in education: the average professor earns more money in a year than the professional athlete earns in a whole week.

Evan Esar

Existentialism means that no one else can take a bath for you.

Delmore Schwartz

I was a fantastic student until the age of ten, but then my mind began to wander.

Grace Paley

An organisation of black academics has been set up to combat racism at universities, polytechnics and colleges of further education. Whites will be excluded.

Steve Race

Food

Food

I eat merely to keep my mind off food.

N. F. Simpson

With this so-called nouvelle cuisine there is nothing on your plate and plenty on your bill.

Paul Bocuse

I don't diet yet I never put on an ounce. I eat six meals a day – four steaks, ten pounds of potatoes, a dozen hamburgers, apple pie, ice-cream and lots of beer. Yet I still weigh the same – twenty-eight stone.

Cyril Smith

I went to a restaurant that serves "breakfast at any time". So I ordered french toast during the Renaissance.

Steven Wright

The baked potatoes looked as though they had been excreted by a buffalo.

Brian Sewell

Too many cooks, in baking rock cakes, get misled by the word "rock".

P. G. Wodehouse

The second day of a diet is easier than the first. By the second day you're off it.

Jackie Gleason

If you travel British Rail with breakfast at King's Cross, lunch in Peterborough and high tea in Doncaster, you will have dinner in hospital.

Victor Lewis-Smith

"I am the emperor and I want dumplings." This was the most lucid utterance of Ferdinand the First.

A. J. P. Taylor

I'm a light eater. As soon as it's light I start to eat.

Art Donovan

I went to South Africa only because I could no longer stand English cold mutton.

Cecil Rhodes

How to eat spinach like a child. Divide into piles. Rearrange again into piles. After five or six manoeuvres, sit back and say you are full.

Delia Ephron

A nuclear power plant is infinitely safer than eating because three hundred people choke to death on food every year.

Dixy Lee Ray

I wouldn't give somebody my last Rolo if they were in a diabetic coma.

Jo Brand

Food

Cooking a crocodile is easy. You need two pots of boiling water, one for the crocodile and one for a rock. By the time the rock is tender, the crocodile will be cooked.

Paul Hogan

Finish your vegetables! There are thousands of children in Hollywood with eating disorders.

John Callaghan

In restaurants, the hardness of the butter increases in direct proportion to the softness of the bread being served.

Harriet Markman

Great restaurants are nothing but mouth-brothels.

Frederic Raphael

As life's pleasures go, food is second only to sex. Except for salami and eggs. Now that's better than sex, but only if the salami is thickly sliced.

Alan King

If this is coffee, please bring me some tea; if this is tea, please bring me some coffee.

Abraham Lincoln

Ostrich tastes like the progeny of an unnatural and uncomfortable liaison between a duck and a sheep.

A.A. Gill

Food

Reality may not be the best of all possible worlds but it's still the only place where you can get a decent steak.

Woody Allen

There are two absolute dining rules: never ever have anything to do with a man in a straw boater and never ever put anything in your mouth that has the prefix "hearty" (this applies to women and food).

A.A. Gill

I'm on a diet as my skin doesn't fit me any more.

Erma Bombeck

The only obvious advantage to being an adult is that you can eat your dessert without having eaten your vegetables.

Lisa Alther

I can't cook. I use a smoke alarm as a timer.

Carol Siskind

There is nothing like a morning funeral for sharpening the appetite for lunch.

Arthur Marshall

Custard is a detestable substance produced by a malevolent conspiracy of the hen, the cow and the cook.

Ambrose Bierce

Food

He's a perfectionist. If he was married to Raquel Welch, he'd expect her to cook.

Don Meredith

Man does not live by murder alone. He needs affection, approval, encouragement and, occasionally, a hearty meal.

Alfred Hitchcock

As a breastfeeding mother, you are basically meals on heels.

Kathy Lette

The American poet Lindsay began his career by codifying the ways in which a poet can get a free meal. Here was a seer, here was a man with a strong grasp of essentials.

Christopher Morley

Zee always went naked in the house, except for the brassiere she wore when it was her turn to get dinner. Once cooking French-fried pototoes in a kettle of boiling fat, she had come within an inch of crisping her most striking features.

G. S. Albee

The Hotel Carvery – as much gristle and cornflour as you can stuff down for a tenner.

A. A. Gill

I've tried to lose weight but I've always had this problem with my feet. I can't keep them out of the fish and chip shop.

Roy Brown

Grub first: then ethics.

Bertolt Brecht

Mosquitos see Elizabeth Taylor and shout "buffet".

Joan Rivers

If a fly gets into the throat of one who is fasting, it is not necessary to pull it out.

Ayatollah Khomeini

Some people sterilize a sweet dropped on the floor by blowing on it, somehow assuming this will remove the germs.

Diana Kent

Consider going on a diet if there a is restraining order against you from the Association of All-You-Can-Eat Restaurants.

J. R. Miller

Time is an illusion, lunchtime doubly so.

Douglas Adams

There is no such thing as a little garlic.

Arthur Baer

You don't eat Mexican food – you just rent it.

Alexei Sayle

Men like to barbecue. Men like to cook only if danger is involved.

Rita Rudner

Food

I'm such an optimist I'd go after Moby Dick in a rowboat
and take the tartar sauce with me.

Zig Ziglar

I'm that hungry I could eat a nun's arse through the convent
railings.

Lily Savage

Give me a kitchen full of utensils and a stock of unprepared
food and I would starve.

Michel De Montaigne

The better a pie tastes, the worse it is for you.

Edgar Howe

Ask your child what he wants for dinner only if he's buying.

Fran Lebowitz

A fork is an instrument used chiefly for the purpose of
putting dead animals into the mouth.

Ambrose Bierce

It was as thin as the homeopathic soup that was made by
boiling the shadow of a pigeon that had starved to death.

Abraham Lincoln

Food

We were taken to a fast food cafe where our order was fed into a computer. Our hamburgers, made from the flesh of chemically impregnated cattle, had been broiled over counterfeit charcoal, placed between slices of artificially flavoured cardboard and served to us by recycled juvenile delinquents.

Jean-Michel Chapereau

When I makes tea I makes tea, as old mother Grogan said, and when I makes water I makes water.

James Joyce

Love is a word properly applied to our delight in particular kinds of food; it is sometimes metaphorically spoken of the favourite objects of all our appetites.

Henry Fielding

I'd like to throw up but the room is too small.

Richard Pryor

I do not like broccoli and I haven't liked it since I was a little kid and my mother made me eat it. Now I'm President of the United States and I'm not going to eat any more broccoli.

George Bush

Lawyers and other Professions

Lawyers and other Professions

Whoever said that talk was cheap never hired a lawyer.

Wayne Mackey

Our experts describe you as an appallingly dull fellow, unimaginative, timid, spineless, easily dominated, no sense of humour, tedious company and irrepressibly drab and awful. And whereas in most professions these would be considered drawbacks, in accountancy they are a positive boon.

John Cleese

I was never ruined but twice: once when I lost a law-suit and once when I won one.

Voltaire

If you cannot get your lawyer to call you, try not paying his bill.

Pete Ferguson

Military intelligence is a contradiction in terms.

Oswald G. Villard

I do not wish to speak ill of any man behind his back, but I believe that gentleman is a lawyer.

Samuel Johnson

A disastrous probate case for a lawyer is when some of the heirs get nearly as much as he does.

John Mortimer

Lawyers and other Professions

Ignorance of the law must not prevent the losing lawyer from collecting his fee.

John Mortimer

In 1939 an attorney in an Oklahoma court sang Home, Sweet Home! to beg for mercy for his bank robber client. The jury promptly brought in a sentence of life imprisonment.

Percy A. Scholes

Juries scare me. I don't want to put my faith in people who weren't smart enough to get out of jury duty.

Monica Piper

God may help those who help themselves but the courts are rough as hell on shoplifters.

Leo Rosten

Journalism is the only thinkable alternative to working.

Jeffrey Bernard

The efficiency of our criminal jury system is marred only by the difficulty of finding twelve men every day who do not know anything and cannot read.

Mark Twain

Richard Nixon, Gary Hart and Teddy Kennedy have just got together to form a new law firm. It's called Trickem, Dickem and Dunkem.

Buffy Bluechip

Lawyers and other Professions

I chose the profession of a burglar because the hours suited me.

Harry Vickers

The screws who work in prisons are usually inadequate and if society didn't keep them in jail they could be a real danger to the public.

Charlie Richardson

Dinny Meehan was the only crime boss I can remember who died in bed. By that I mean that somebody slipped in through his bedroom window while he was asleep and put a bullet in his brain.

Willy Sutton

Equality under the law forbids the rich as well as the poor to sleep under bridges, to beg in the streets and to steal bread.

Anatole France

I haven't committed a crime. All I did was fail to comply with the law.

David Dinkins

We live in an age when pizza gets to your house before the police do.

Jeff Marder

A jury is a group of twelve people who, having lied to the judge about their hearing, health and business engagements, have failed to fool him.

H. L. Mencken

Lawyers and other Professions

I used to be a lawyer, but now I am a reformed character.
Woodrow Wilson

There is no police like Holmes.
James Joyce

Lawyers make a living out of trying to figure out what other lawyers have written.
Will Rogers

A majority is that quality that distinguishes a crime from a law.
Ambrose Bierce

After you've heard two eye witness accounts of an accident, it makes you wonder about history.
Dave Barry

The minute you read something that you can't understand, you can almost be sure it was written by lawyers.
Will Rogers

Pipe smokers spend so much time cleaning, filling and fooling around with their pipes they don't have any time to break the law.
Bill Vaughan

I have lied in good faith.
Bernard Tapie

If I want your opinion, I'll give it to you.

Al Capone

Eye witnesses were on the scene in minutes.

Adam Boulton

I learned law so well, the day I graduated I sued the college and got my tuition fees back.

Fred Allen

I'm for a stronger death penalty.

George Bush

When I was young I looked like Al Capone, but I lacked his compassion.

Oscar Levant

Someday son you'll meet somebody very special. Someone who won't press charges.

Raul Julia

Literature

Truman Capote's death was a good career move.

Gore Vidal

Would you convey my compliments to the purist who reads your proofs and tell him or her that I write in a sort of broken-down patois which is something like the way a Swiss waiter talks and that when I split an infinitive, God dammit, I split it so it will stay split.

Raymond Chandler

Poor Matthew Arnold, he's gone to heaven no doubt – but he won't like God.

Robert Louis Stevenson

That writer is so bad he shouldn't be left alone in a room with a typewriter.

Herman J. Manciewicz

An author is a fool who, not content with having bored those who have lived with him, insists on boring future generations.

Charles De Secondat

The only reason I didn't kill myself after I read the reviews of my first book was because we have two rivers in New York and I couldn't decide which one to jump into.

Wilfred Sheed

No poet or novelist wishes he were the only one who ever lived but most of them wish they were the only one alive and quite a few fondly believe their wish has been granted.

W. H. Auden

Literature

Lord Byron had just two commandments – hate your neighbour and love your neighbour's wife.

Thomas B. Macaulay

Though he tortures the English language, he has never yet succeeded in forcing it to reveal its meaning.

J. B. Morton

It will take a special dispensation from Heaven to get H. L. Mencken into the deepest pit in Hell.

Hugh Jackson

I would sooner read a timetable or a catalogue than nothing at all. They are much more entertaining than half the novels written.

Somerset Maugham

God cannot alter the past. That is why He had to create so many historians.

Samuel Butler

In writing a novel, when in doubt, have two guys come through the door with guns.

Raymond Chandler

Chuang Tzu was born in the fourth century B.C. The publication of this book in English, over two thousand years after his death, is obviously premature.

Bernard Levin

Henry Miller is not really a writer but a non-stop talker to whom someone has given a typewriter.

Gerald Brenan

In real life, of course, it is the hare who wins. Every time. Look around you. And in any case, it is my contention that Aesop was writing for the tortoise market.

Anita Brookner

I have nothing to say, I am saying it and that is poetry.

John Cage

I do not think that Rousseau's poem "Ode to Posterity" will reach its destination.

Voltaire

Every good journalist has a novel in him – which is an excellent place for it.

Russell Lynes

Everywhere I go, I am asked if I think the university stifles writers. My opinion is that it doesn't stifle enough of them.

Flannery O'Connor

Autobiography is an unrivalled vehicle for telling the truth about other people.

Philip Guedalla

The only demand I make of my reader is that he should devote his whole life to reading my works.

James Joyce

This is a book everyone can afford to be without.

Edmund Crispin

There's a new dictionary for masochists. It has all the words but they're not in alphabetical order.

Frank Tyger

A historian is just an unsuccessful novelist.

H. L. Mencken

Proof-reading is more effective after publication.

Eric Barker

The value of rubbish is unaltered by translation, abstraction or citation.

Dennis Gunton

You could always tell by his conversation which volume of Encyclopaedia Britannica Aldous Huxley had been reading. One day it would be Alps, Andes and Apennines and the next it would be the Himalayas and the Hippocratic Oath.

Bertrand Russell

I enjoyed talking to Virginia Woolf, but thought nothing of her writing. I considered her a beautiful little knitter.

Edith Sitwell

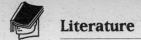

Literature

My book *Auntie Mame* circulated for five years, through the halls of fifteen publishers and finally ended up with Vanguard Press, which, as you can see, is rather deep into the alphabet.

Patrick Dennis

One could always baffle Conrad by saying "humour".

H. G. Wells

You ask if I keep a copy of every book I print. Madam, I keep thousands.

Jonathan Cape

Only ambitious nonentities and hearty mediocrities exhibit their rough drafts. It's like passing around samples of one's sputum.

Vladimir Nabokov

Jane Austen's books, too, are absent from this library. Just that one omission alone would make a fairly good library out of a library that hadn't a book in it.

Mark Twain

All my major works have been written in prison. I would recommend prison not only to aspiring writers but to aspiring politicians too.

Jawaharlal Nehru

Meredith is a prose Browning, and so is Browning.

Oscar Wilde

I hate vulgar realism in literature. The man who would call a spade a spade should be compelled to use one. It is the only thing he is fit for.

Oscar Wilde

The only trouble with Seamus O'Sullivan is that when he's not drunk he's sober.

W. B. Yeats

John Cole's book is a strangely old fashioned work, of the kind that used to be written in the 1920s by authors with such pseudonyms as A Gentleman With A Duster.

Anthony Howard

This book is the best work of fiction since fidelity was included in the French marriage vows.

Rowan Atkinson

I do not think the expenditure of $2.50 for a book entitles the purchaser to the personal friendship of the author.

Evelyn Waugh

A magnum opus is a book which when dropped from a three storey building is big enough to kill a man.

Edward Wilson

What every author really wants is to have letters printed in the newspaper. Unable to make the grade, he drops down a rung of the ladder and writes novels.

P. G. Wodehouse

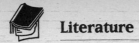

Southern [American] literature can be summed up in these words: "On the night the hogs ate Willy, Mama died when she heard what Daddy did to sister."

Pat Conroy

I asked my publisher what would happen if he sold all the copies of my book he had printed. He said "I'll just print another ten."

Eric Sykes

I have always wanted to write a book that ended with the word "mayonnaise".

Richard Brautigan

I don't do much book reviewing anymore. It interferes too much with my reading.

Dorothy Parker

George Russell's only fault was his inability to distinguish between turbot and halibut.

George Moore

I have been commissioned by Michael Joseph to write my autobiography. Can anyone tell me where I was between 1960 and 1974 and what the hell was I doing?

Jeffrey Bernard

A better case for the banning of all poetry is the simple fact that it is bad. Nobody is going to manufacture a thousand tons of jam in the expectation that five tons of it may be eatable.

Flann O'Brien

God created the Poet and then took a handful of the rubbish that was left and made three critics.

T. J. Thomas

Anybody who can write home for money can write for magazines.

Wilson Mizner

Half the sucess of Marie Corelli is due to the no doubt unfounded rumour that she is a woman.

Oscar Wilde

Poets have been mysteriously silent on the subject of cheese.

G. K. Chesterton

Asking a working writer what he thinks about critics is like asking a lamp post how it feels about dogs.

Christopher Hampton

The writing of Robert Montgomery bears the same relation to poetry as a Turkish carpet bears to a picture. There are colours in the carpet out of which a picture might be made. There are words in Mr. Montgomery's verses which, when disposed in certain orders and combinations, have made and will again make good poetry.

Thomas B. Macaulay

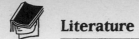

Literature

In this edition of *The Coral Island* printed in Russia some of the author's impressions have been curtailed or omitted and the episodes after the three heroes get away from the island have been dropped as being in the nature of an anticlimax. The book as a story is improved by their omission.

Peter Haddock

If a young writer can refrain from writing, he shouldn't hesitate to do so.

André Gide

Suicide attempts and then writing poems about your suicide attempts is just pure bullshit.

James Dickey

I am writing an unauthorised autobiography.

Steven Wright

Steele might become a reasonably good writer if he would pay a little more attention to grammar, learn something about the propriety and disposition of words and, incidentally, get some information on the subject he intends to handle.

Jonathan Swift

I do thirty-seven drafts of every story I write. I once tried thirty-three but something was lacking, a certain – how shall I say? – *je ne sais quoi*. On another occasion, I tried forty-two versions, but the final effect was too lapidary – do you know what I mean, Jack?

S. J. Perelman

Make the reader laugh and he will think you a trivial fellow,
but bore him in the right way and your reputation is assured.

Somerset Maugham

A man who has never been within the tropics does not
know what a thunderstorm means; a man who has never
looked on Niagara has but a faint idea of a cataract; and he
who has not read Barere's *Memoirs* may be said not to know
what it is to lie.

Thomas B. Macaulay

Never buy an editor or publisher a lunch or a drink until he
has bought an article, story or book from you. This rule is
absolute and may be broken at your peril.

John Creasey

I don't really start until I get my proofs back from the
printers. Then I can begin serious writing.

J. M. Keynes

This book fills a much needed gap.

Moses Hadas

Sometimes when reading Goethe I have the paralysing
suspicion that he is trying to be funny.

Guy Davenport

I put a million monkeys on typewriters to see if they would
type the works of Shakespeare, but all I got was the *Collected
Works of Francis Bacon*.

Bill Hirst

Literature

Dave Barry is the best known, best liked and most successful humour writer in the United States. We would call him "beloved" if only he were older and had a fatal disease.

P. J. O'Rourke

All Shakespeare did was to string together a lot of old well known quotations.

H. L. Mencken

I was reading the dictionary the other day. I thought it was a poem about everything.

Steven Wright

The covers of this book are too far apart.

Ambrose Bierce

Although most magazines pay so much a word, virtually none of them will be words submitted individually.

Edward Morris

My eventual aim is to be recognised first as a man and eventually as author, poet and philosopher.

Reggie Kray

Some day I hope to write a book where the royalties will pay for the copies I give away.

Clarence Darrow

The secret of writing great literature is to be under house arrest.

Georg Lukacs

George Moore leads his readers to the latrine and locks them in.

Oscar Wilde

This is the best book ever written by any man on the wrong side of a question of which he is profoundly ignorant.

Thomas B. Macaulay

A collaboration is a literary partnership based on the false assumption that the other fellow can spell.

Ambrose Bierce

Homer is dead, Dante is dead, Shakespeare is dead and I'm not feeling too well myself.

Artemus Ward

When audiences come to see us authors lecture, it is in the hope that we'll be funnier to look at than to read.

Sinclair Lewis

I called my first book "The Collected Works of Max Beerbohm, Volume One".

Max Beerbohm

Teenagers are interesting for many reasons – for their sex lives, their unshakable belief in the suitability of jeans for every social occasion – but one thing you pass on, politely but firmly, is their poetry.

Tom Shone

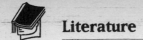

Literature

You can get away with saying anything stupid, as long as you attribute it to Samuel Johnson, Marcus Aurelius or Dorothy Parker.

George Mikes

In the beginning was the review copy and a man received it from the publisher. Then he wrote a review. Then he wrote a book which the publisher accepted and sent on to someone else as a review copy. The man who received it did likewise. This is how modern literature came into being.

Karl Kraus

I hate authors. I wouldn't mind them so much if they didn't write books.

Polly Walker

Macaulay improves. I have observed in him, of late, flashes of silence.

Sydney Smith

I told the priest in the confessional that I had committed plagiarism and he asked me if it was alone or with somebody else.

Kevin Dillon

The dubious privilege of a freelance writer is that he's given the freedom to starve anywhere.

S. J. Perelman

Living — Family and Relations

Death is a wonderful way of cutting down on your expenses.
Woody Allen

The luckiest man in the world was Adam – he had no mother-in-law.
Sholom Aleichem

I refuse to admit I'm more than fifty-two even if that does make my sons illegitimate.
Nancy Astor

Any child who is anxious to mow the lawn is too young to do it.
Bob Phillips

Some parents have difficulty deciding on a name for the new baby, but others have rich relatives.
Don McElroy

The main purpose of children's parties is to remind you that there are children worse than your own.
Katharine Whitehorn

Everybody wants to save the earth – nobody wants to help Mom to do the dishes.
P. J. O'Rourke

George Orwell was virtually an only child – one sister was five years older, the other five years younger.
Stephen Wadhams

My father used to go round in some peculiar circles – one of his legs was shorter than the other.

Rick Mayall

Big sisters are the crabgrass in the lawn of life.

Charles M. Schultz

When my time comes to die, I want to go quietly and with dignity like my daddy and not screaming and roaring like his passengers.

Pat O'Brien

You can help solve the overpopulation problem this quick easy way! This year, why not commit suicide? Just leave a note telling your loved ones that you did it to help stave off worldwide famine and they will respect and admire you for your courage.

Robert Crumb

When my kids become wild and unruly, I use a nice safe playpen. When they're finished, I climb out.

Erma Bombeck

Here's a motto for all breastfeeding mothers – there's a little sucker born every minute – thanks for the mammaries.

Dominic Cleary

As a teenager you are in the last stage of life when you will be happy to hear that the phone is for you.

Fran Lebowitz

It is not advisable to put your head around your child's door to see if it is asleep. It was.

Faith Hines

Self-esteem is a good thing but anyone who has ever toilet trained a child knows that it is possible to make too much of the efforts of the child on the potty. One wonders if little Ed Koch was told once too often what a great thing he'd done and began to think that all that emanated from his being was pretty great.

Peggy Noonan

My family was so poor the lady next door gave birth to me.

Lee Trevino

Saving is a fine thing. Especially when your parents have done it for you.

Winston Churchill

The more keys a household owns, the more frequently will members of the family lock themselves out.

Faith Hines

My parents stayed together for forty years but that was out of spite.

Woody Allen

Any small child is capable of calculating that his tousled appearance at the height of a party will draw enough applause from the unmarried women present to win him at least half an hour out of bed and a biscuit.

Faith Hines

Every family should have at least three children. Then if one is a genius the other two can support him.

George Coote

I will not allow my daughters to learn foreign languages because one tongue is sufficient for a woman.

John Milton

Princess Margaret is the Billy Carter of the British monarchy.

Robert Lacey

Don't worry about senility — when it hits you, you won't know it.

Bill Cosby

There is nothing wrong with the younger generation that becoming a taxpayer won't cure.

Dan Bennett

He's a good boy; everything he steals he brings right home to his mother.

Fred Allen

When they come up with a riding vacuum cleaner, then I'll clean the house.

Roseanne Barr

I was quite enjoying *The Power of Positive Thinking*, until I heard that the author had committed suicide.

Nick Job

Living — Family and Relations

Only a friend can become an enemy. A relative is one from the start.

Harry Hershfield

He was a good family man. Everywhere he went he started a new family.

Liam O'Reilly

When I was born folks came from miles around to take a look. They weren't quite sure what the little thing was.

W. C. Fields

I don't approve of smacking children — I just use a cattle prod.

Jenny Eclair

Some families have skeletons in the closet — with us the skeletons have the run of the house and we live in the closet.

Joe McCarroll

Be nice to your children. After all, they are going to choose your nursing home.

Steven Wright

I am absolutely sure there is no life on Mars — it's not listed on my teenage daughter's phone bills.

Larry Mathews

I have never understood the fear of some parents about babies getting mixed up in the hospital. What difference does it make so long as you get a good one?

Heywood Broun

Every household has a box of odd keys. None of them will ever be found to fit any lock.

Pam Brown

The trouble with incest is that it gets you involved with relatives.

George S. Kaufman

My wife is an excellent creature, but she can never remember which came first, the Greeks or the Romans.

Benjamin Disraeli

What is the advantage of having a kid at forty-nine? So you can both be in diapers at the same time?

Sue Kolinsky

We are none of us infallible: not even the youngest of us.

W. H. Thompson

I am a hundred and two years of age. I have no worries since my youngest son went into an old folks' home.

Victoria Bedwell

A married man with a family will do anything for money.

Talleyrand

Perhaps host and guest is really the happiest relation for father and son.

Evelyn Waugh

The moment you have children yourself, you forgive your parents everything.

Susan Hill

If you've never seen a real, fully developed look of disgust, tell your son how you conducted yourself when you were a boy.

Kin Hubbard

I played Find the Lady with my gambling friends one boozy night by shuffling my infant triplets – only one of whom was female – on the sofa.

Richard Hannon

When our phone rings it's always for our daughter. When it isn't ringing it's because she's talking on it. Sometimes when she's on our phone the neighbours will come over and tell her she's wanted on their phone.

Art Frank

Fathers should be neither seen nor heard. That is the only proper basis for family life.

Oscar Wilde

There's nothing wrong with teenagers that reasoning with them won't aggravate.

Jean Kerr

I take my children everywhere but they always find their way home again.

Robert Orben

My father was frightened of his father, I was frightened of my father and I am damn well going to see to it that my children are frightened of me.

King George V

Any mother could perform the jobs of several air traffic controllers with ease.

Lisa Alther

We cannot start our married life with thirteen children. It would be most unlucky.

H. H. Munro

Children are nature's very own form of birth control.

Dave Barry

My father died when I was eight. At least that's what he told us in the letter.

Drew Carey

This book is dedicated to my mother, Mrs. Frieda Seidman; to my daughters, Laurie Jo and Mona Helene; and to my wife Sylvia. All equally dear to me, but for safety's sake listed here alphabetically according to first name.

Gerald F. Lieberman

Many authorities now feel that W. C. Fields was right about kids.

Robert Byrne

I want to have children but my friends scare me. One of them told me she was in labour for thirty-six hours. I don't even want to do something that feels good for thirty-six hours.

Rita Rudner

Adolescence is that period in a kid's life when parents become more difficult.

Ryan O'Neal

People who say they sleep like a baby usually don't have one.

Leo J. Burke

Children despise their parents until the age of forty, when they suddenly become just like them, thus preserving the system.

Quentin Crewe

I am fond of all children except boys.

Lewis Carroll

Many a man wishes he were strong enough to tear a telephone book in half – especially if he has a teenage daughter.

Guy Lombardo

A suburban mother's role is to deliver children; obstetrically once and by car forever after.

Peter de Vries

If a man smiles at home somebody is sure to ask him for money.

William Feather

We spend our lives on the run: we get up by the clock, eat and sleep by the clock, get up again, go to work – and then we retire. And what do they give us? A bloody clock.

Dave Allen

How often does a house need to be cleaned anyway? Just once every girlfriend. After that she can get to know the real you.

P. J. O'Rourke

My grandmother made dying her life's work.

Hugh Leonard

At the unemployment exchange my father gave his occupation as an astronaut but not prepared to travel.

Roy Brown

Procrastination is the art of keeping up with yesterday.

Don Marquis

Any child's birthday party in which the number of guests exceeds the number of the actual age of the child for whom the party is being given will end in disaster.

Pierre Burton

Do not join encounter groups. If you enjoy being made to feel inadequate, call your mother.

Liz Smith

My mother-in-law's face is her fortune. She pays no income tax.

Les Dawson

He'll regret it to his dying day, if ever he lives that long.

Frank Nugent

My brother and I devoted all our boyhood to one long argument, unfortunately interrupted by meals, school and work.

G. K. Chesterton

When I turned two I was really anxious, because I'd doubled my age in a year. I thought, if this keeps up, by the time I'm seven I'll be over a hundred.

Wright Stevens

My mother had a great deal of trouble with me, but I think she enjoyed it.

Mark Twain

Dear Mrs., Mr., Miss or Mr. and Mrs.; Words cannot express the deep personal grief I experienced when your husband, son, father or brother was killed, wounded or reported missing in action.

Joseph Heller

I will always remember the last words of my grandfather who said, "A truck!"

Emo Philips

Homosexuality is God's way of ensuring that the truly gifted aren't burdened with children.

Sam Austin

If the garbage man calls, tell him we don't want any.

Groucho Marx

Never change diapers in mid stream.

Don Marquis

One of the first things you notice about a backward country is the way children obey their parents.

Erma Bombeck

Poverty is hereditary – you get it from your children.

Phyllis Diller

The art of negotiation is something you learn at an early age. You'd be amazed how many teenagers get their first car by asking for a motorcycle.

James Hewett

If you don't learn to laugh at trouble, you won't have anything to laugh at when you're old.

Edgar Howe

All you need to grow fine vigorous grass is a crack in your sidewalk.

James Hewett

Universal peace sounds ridiculous to the head of the average family.

Kin Hubbard

Have a place for everything and keep the thing somewhere else; this is not a piece of advice, it is merely a custom.

Mark Twain

Why not give your son a motorcycle for his last birthday?

Colin Bowles

I'm 42 around the chest, 52 around the waist, 92 around the golf course and a nuisance around the house.

Groucho Marx

Every man sees in his relatives, and especially his cousins, a series of grotesque caricatures of himself.

H. L. Mencken

As a parent, I do everything except breastfeeding.

Andy Gray

There are many things you can learn from children — like how much patience you have for instance.

Fran Lebowitz

I wasn't born in a slum, but my family moved into one as soon as we could afford it.

Melville Landon

Living — Family and Relations

It is one of the great urban myths that people get pregnant in order to have children.

Menzies Campbell

I tried to run away from home at the age of ten months.

Oscar Levant

If you must choose between living with your mother-in-law and blowing out your brains, do not hesitate – blow out hers.

Victorien Sardou

Suicide is belated acquiescence to the opinion of one's wife's relatives.

H. L. Mencken

Even when freshly washed and relieved of all obvious confections, children tend to be sticky.

Fran Lebowitz

I've never told this to anyone before, but when I was a baby, I was breastfed from falsies.

Woody Allen

Every day I get up at the crack of noon.

Lucille Ball

If thine enemy offend thee, give his child a drum.

Fran Lebowitz

Don't try to make children grow up to be like you or they may do it.

Russell Baker

If you live to be one hundred you've got it made. Very few people die past that age.

George Burns

Children and grandparents get along so well together because they have the same enemy – the mother.

Claudette Colbert

Go back to reform school, you little nose picker.

W. C. Fields

Love, Sex, Marriage, Men and Women

A man with pierced ears is better prepared for marriage. He
has experienced pain and bought jewellery.

Rita Rudner

Only a flaw of fate prevented Vita Sackville-West from being
one of nature's gentlemen.

Edith Sitwell

Women are a problem, but they are the kind of problem I
enjoy wrestling with.

Warren Beatty

It takes a real man to wear make-up.

Rikki Rocket

The useless piece of flesh at the end of a penis is called a
man.

Jo Brand

A loving wife will do anything for her husband except to
stop criticizing and trying to improve him.

J. B. Priestley

Of course I believe in safe sex – I've got a handrail around
the bed.

To win a woman in the first place you must please her, then
undress her, and then somehow get her clothes back on her,
finally, so that she will let you leave her, you've got to
antagonise her.

Jean Giradoux

The major achievement of the women's movement in the nineteen-seventies was the Dutch treat.

Nora Ephron

It's so tiring making love to women, it takes forever. I'm too lazy to be a lesbian.

Camille Paglia

You don't know how difficult it has been being a closet heterosexual.

David Bowie

Nothing is more distasteful to me than that entire complacency and satisfaction which beam in the countenances of a new married couple.

Charles Lamb

When people say "You're breaking my heart", they do in fact mean that you're breaking their genitals.

Jeffrey Bernard

Every man I meet wants to protect me. I can't figure out from what.

Mae West

The fulminations of the missionaries about sex in Listowel will have as little effect as the droppings of an underweight blackbird on the water-level of the Grand Coulee Dam.

Eamon Keane

The mini-skirt enables young ladies to run faster and because of it, they may have to.

John V. Lindsay

Brigands demand your money or your life – women require both.

Samuel Butler

I have half a mind to get married – and that's all I need.

Bob Phillips

My wife met me at the door wearing a see-through negligee. Unfortunately, she was just coming home.

Rodney Dangerfield

Teenage boys, goaded by their hormones, run in packs like the primal horde. They have only a brief season of exhilarating liberty between control by their mothers and control by their wives.

Camille Paglia

Women's liberation will not be achieved until a woman can become paunchy and bald and still think she's attractive to the opposite sex.

Earl Wilson

A man's womenfolk, whatever their outward show of respect for his merit and authority, always regard him secretly as an ass, and with something akin to pity.

H. L. Mencken

Every woman needs at least three men: one for sex, one for money and one for fun.

Bess Myerson

Suburban Chicago is virgin territory for whorehouses.

Al Capone

On quiet nights, when I am alone, I like to run our wedding video backwards, just to watch myself walk out of the church a free man.

George Coote

Men should think again about making widowhood women's only path to power.

Gloria Steinem

If you think women are the weaker sex, try pulling the blankets back to your side.

Stuart Turner

No woman has ever shot her husband while he was doing the dishes.

George Coote

Never feel remorse for what you have thought about your wife; she has thought much worse things about you.

Jean Rostand

Edward Kennedy has just gone on his honeymoon. Now he'll be able to do something he's never been able to do before – check into a hotel under his own name.

Jay Leno

A woman's place is in the wrong.

James Thurber

Instead of getting married again, I'm going to find a woman I don't like and give her a house.

Lewis Grizzard

All the unhappy marriages come from husbands having brains. What good are brains to a man? They only unsettle him.

P. G. Wodehouse

A homely face and no figure have aided many a woman heavenward.

Minna Antrim

All the world loves a lover – unless he's in a telephone booth.

Dave Tomick

Pandora and I are in love! It is official! She told Claire Neilson, who told Nigel who told me.

Adrian Mole

There is little wife-swopping in suburbia. It is unnecessary, the females all being so similar.

Richard Gordon

Funny how a wife can spot a blonde hair at twenty yards, yet miss the garage doors.

Corey Ford

If a man stays away from his wife for seven years, the law presumes the separation to have killed him; yet according to our daily experience, it might well prolong his life.

Charles Darling

The best way to get a husband to do anything is to suggest that he is too old to do it.

Shirley MacLaine

I can always find plenty of women to sleep with me but the kind of woman that is really hard for me to find is a typist who can read my writing.

Thomas Wolfe

For certain people, after fifty, litigation takes the place of sex.

Gore Vidal

A woman is the second most important item in a bedroom.

Paul Hogan

This book is dedicated to my brilliant and beautiful wife without whom I would be nothing. She always comforts and consoles, never complains or interferes, asks nothing and endures all. She also writes my dedications.

Albert Malvino

Love, Sex, Marriage...

My sex life is now reduced to fan letters from an elderly lesbian who wants to borrow $800.

Groucho Marx

Marry me Dorothy and you'll be farting through silk.

Robert Mitchum

I met the ornithology correspondent of the *Irish Times*, a very prim and proper lady, one cold winter's afternoon and I said to her: "How's the blue tits today, missus?"

Brendan Behan

A bore is a man in love with another woman.

Mary Poole

A man will marry a woman because he needs a mother he can communicate with.

Martin Mull

She is in love with her own husband – monstrous, what a selfish woman.

Jennie Churchill

A husband should tell his wife everything that he is sure she will find out anyway and before anybody else does.

Thomas Dewar

I'm quite happy with my mistress. She goes to bed with others because she loves them, but for money – only with me.

Ferenc Molnar

Love, Sex, Marriage...

Telling a teenager the facts of life is like giving a fish a bath.
Arnold Glasow

Never despise what it says in the women's magazines: it may not be subtle but neither are the men.
Zsa-Zsa Gabor

At eighty-two, I feel like a twenty-year-old, but unfortunately, there's never one around.
Milton Berle

Never trust a man with testicles.
Jo Brand

A very little wit is valued in a woman, as we are pleased with a few words spoken plain by a parrot.
Jonathan Swift

Marriage is but for a little while. It is alimony that is forever.
Quentin Crisp

There are four sexes: men, women, clergymen and journalists.
Somerset Maugham

The only way to get rid of cockroaches is to tell them you want a long-term relationship.
Jasmine Birtles

Men don't know anything about pain; they have never experienced labour, cramps or a bikini wax.

Nan Tisdale

How do I feel about men? With my fingers.

Cher

I have frequently been faithful to my wife.

Gerald Kennedy

In our family, we don't divorce our men – we bury them.

Ruth Gordon

The trouble is you can't live with men, but then you can't chop them into little pieces and boil the flesh off their bones, because that would be cooking.

Jenny Eclair

She was a freelance castrator.

James Thurber

It's a funny thing that when a man hasn't got anything on earth to worry about he goes off and gets married.

Robert Frost

The best part of married life is the fights. The rest is so-so.

Thornton Wilder

Man is the second strangest sex in the world.

Philip Barry

I love being married. It's so great to find the one special person you want to annoy for the rest of your life.

Rita Rudner

My husband claims to be a great sexual athlete, just because he always comes first.

Ellie Lane

In a world without men, there would be no crime and a lot of fat happy women.

Nicole Hollander

Marriage is a sort of friendship recognised by the police.

Robert Louis Stevenson

Sex is essentially just a matter of good lighting.

Noel Coward

Teenagers are God's punishment for having sex.

Patrick Murray

From where she parked the car it was just a short walk to the footpath.

Woody Allen

The Miss World Contest has always had its fair share of knockers.

Julia Morley

The only difference about being married is that you don't have to get out of bed to fart.

Jimmy Goldsmith

One of the advantages of living alone is that you don't have to wake up in the arms of a loved one.

Marion Smith

If you want sex, have an affair. If you want a relationship, buy a dog.

Julie Burchill

Once women made it public that they could do things better than men, they were of course forced to do precisely that. So now they have to be elected to political office and get jobs as officers of major corporations and so on, instead of ruling the world by batting their eyelids the way they used to.

P. J. O'Rourke

Sex hasn't been the same since women started to enjoy it.

Lewis Grizzard

Think of me as a sex symbol for the man who doesn't give a damn.

Phyllis Diller

My mother said it was simple to keep a man. You must be a maid in the living room, a cook in the kitchen and a whore in the bedroom. I said I'd hire the first two and take care of the bedroom bit myself.

Jerry Hall

The difference between sex and death is with death you can get to do it alone and nobody's going to make fun of you.

Woody Allen

This book is dedicated to all those men who betrayed me at one time or another, in the hopes that they will fall off their motorcycles and break their necks.

Diane Wakoski

The hardest task in a girl's life is to prove to a man that his intentions are serious.

Helen Rowland

Of course a platonic relationship is possible, but only between a husband and wife.

Irving Kristol

Mrs. Williams has never yet let her husband finish a sentence since his "I will", at Trinity Church, Plymouth Dock in 1782.

Patrick O'Brian

There is one thing women can never take away from men. We die sooner.

P. J. O'Rourke

They caught the first female serial killer, but she didn't kill the men herself. She gained access to their apartments, hid their remote controls and they killed themselves.

Elayne Boosler

I was the first woman to burn my bra – it took the fire department four days to put it out.

Dolly Parton

There are three intolerable things in life – cold coffee, lukewarm champagne and overexcited women.

Orson Welles

Marriage always demands the greatest understanding of the art of insincerity possible between two human beings.

Vicki Baum

I've been married so long I'm on my third bottle of Tabasco sauce.

Susan Vass

The night of our honeymoon my husband took one look and said, "Is that all for me?".

Dolly Parton

Teenage girls can get pregnant merely by standing downwind of teenage boys.

Dave Barry

A broken heart is what makes life so wonderful five years later, when you see the guy in the elevator and he is fat and smoking a cigar and saying long-time-no-see. If he had not broken your heart you could not have that glorious feeling of relief.

Phyllis Battelle

If you had suggested to primitive man that they should watch women having babies, they would have laughed and tortured you for three or four days.

Dave Barry

I was into animal husbandry – until they caught me at it.

Tom Lehrer

Women dress alike all over the world; they dress to be annoying to other women.

Elsa Schiaparelli

The roses and raptures of vice are damned uncomfortable as you will soon find out. You have to get into such ridiculous positions.

John Mortimer

Whatever happened to the kind of love leech that lived in his car and dropped by once a month to throw up and use you for your shower? Now all the pigs want is a commitment.

Judy Tenuta

Her face was her chaperone.

Rupert Hughes

Some people ask the secret of our long marriage. We take time to go to a restaurant two times a week. A little candlelight, dinner, music and dancing. She goes on Tuesdays. I go Fridays.

Henny Youngman

My wife and I tried to breakfast together but we had to stop or our marriage would have been wrecked.

Winston Churchill

I'm the intelligent, independent-type woman. In other words, a girl who can't get a man.

Shelley Winters

I took up a collection for a man in our office but I didn't get enough money to buy one.

Ruth Buzzi

Elizabeth Taylor married Larry Fortensky, a man younger than her first wedding dress.

A.A. Gill

Meet me in the bedroom in five minutes and bring a cattle prod.

Woody Allen

Married! I can see you now, in the kitchen, bending over a hot stove, but I can't see the stove.

Groucho Marx

All women are stimulated by the news that any wife has left her husband.

Anthony Powell

There is so little difference between husbands you might as well keep the first.

Adela Rogers St. John

In Hollywood the girl throwing the bouquet at a wedding is just as likely to be the next one to marry as the girl who catches it.

Geraldine Page

Have you heard about the woman who stabbed her husband thirty-seven times? I admire her restraint.

Roseanne Barr

More husbands would leave home if they knew how to pack their suitcases.

Leopold Fetchner

Vittorio Gassman used to grab me in his arms, hold me close and tell me how wonderful he was.

Shelley Winters

Don't imagine you can change a man unless he's in nappies.

Jasmine Birtles

Open marriage is nature's way of telling you that you need a divorce.

Marshall Brickman

Never sleep with a man who has named his willy.

Jasmine Birtles

I belong to Bridegrooms Anonymous. Whenever I feel like getting married they send over a lady in housecoat and hair curlers to burn my toast for me.

Dick Martin

The first part of our marriage was very happy. Then, on the way back from the ceremony...

Henny Youngman

People keep asking me if I'll marry again. It's as if after you've had one car crash you want another.

Stephanie Beecham

Never get into a narrow double bed with a wide single man.

Quentin Crisp

When a man makes a woman his wife it's the highest compliment he can pay her and it's usually the last.

Helen Rowland

The only time a woman has a true orgasm is when she is shopping.

Joan Rivers

Remember men, we're fighting for this woman's honour; which is probably more than she ever did.

Groucho Marx

Being a woman is of interest only to aspiring male transsexuals. To actual women, it is simply a good excuse not to play football.

Fran Lebowitz

A man is as old only as the woman he feels.

Groucho Marx

When he's late for dinner, I know he's either having an affair or is lying dead in the street. I always hope it's the street.

Jessica Tandy

I'll believe it when girls of twenty with money marry
paupers turned sixty.

Elbert Hubbard

It's a pity that Marie Stopes' mother had not thought of birth
control.

Muriel Spark

Love. Everyone says that looks don't matter, age doesn't
matter, money doesn't matter. But I never met a girl yet who
has fallen in love with an old ugly man who's broke.

Rodney Dangerfield

I'd much rather be a woman than a man. Women can cry,
they can wear cute clothes – and they're the first to be
rescued off sinking ships.

Gilda Radner

I want a man who is kind and understanding. Is that too
much to ask of a billionaire?

Zsa-Zsa Gabor

Infatuation is when you think he's as sexy as Robert
Redford, as smart as Henry Kissinger, as noble as Ralph
Nader, as funny as Woody Allen and as athletic as Jimmy
Connors. Love is when you realise he's as sexy as Woody
Allen, as smart as Jimmy Connors, as funny as Ralph Nader,
as athletic as Henry Kissinger and nothing like Robert
Redford – but you'll take him anyway.

Judith Viorst

I am not bald – my head is just a solar panel for a sex machine.

Telly Savalas

If women dressed for men, the clothes stores wouldn't sell much – just an occasional sun visor.

Groucho Marx

Anyone who calls it sexual intercourse can't possibly be interested in doing it. You might as well announce you're ready for lunch by proclaiming, "I'd like to do some masticating and enzyme secreting."

Allan Sherman

Sex is a bad thing because it crumples the bedclothes.

Jacqueline Onassis

Leaving sex to the feminists is like letting your dog vacation at the taxidermists.

Camille Paglia

I always run into strong women who are looking for weak men to dominate them.

Andy Warhol

Sleeping with Aldous Huxley was like being crawled over by slugs.

Nancy Cunard

My girlfriend told me she was seeing another man. I told her to rub her eyes.

Emo Philips

You know what I did before I got married? Anything I
wanted to.

Henny Youngman

If God had meant them to be lifted and separated, He would
have put one on each shoulder.

Victoria Woods

From best sellers to comic books, any child who hasn't
acquired an extensive sex education by the age of twelve
belongs in remedial reading.

Will Stanton

The avowed purpose of pornography is to excite sexual
desire which is unnecessary in the case of the young,
inconvenient in the case of the middle aged and impossible
in the case of the old.

Malcolm Muggeridge

If you love a man, set him free. If he comes back, it means
he's forgotten his sandwiches.

Jasmine Birtles

I haven't heard of many girls being attracted by poor old
men.

Sophia Loren

In high school I would have killed for reliable information
on the uterus. But having discussed it at length and seen full
colour diagrams, I must say it has lost much of its charm,
although I still respect it a great deal as an organ.

Dave Barry

Do I lift weights? Sure. Every time I stand up.

Dolly Parton

Boy, am I exhausted. I went on a double date the other night and the other girl didn't turn up.

Mae West

Your spouse should be attractive enough to turn you on. Anything more is trouble.

Albert Brooks

My wife and I have a great relationship. I love sex and she'll do anything to get out of the kitchen.

Milton Berle

I wanted to marry her ever since I saw the moonlight shining on the barrel of her father's shotgun.

Eddie Albert

A man without a woman is like a moose without a hatrack.

Arthur Marshall

There are men I could spend eternity with – but not this life.

Kathleen Norris

I learned about sex from my mother. I asked her where babies came from and she thought I said rabies. She said from a dog bite and a week later a lady on our block gave birth to triplets. I thought she had been bitten by a Great Dane.

Woody Allen

When I got back from my third honeymoon, I just couldn't understand why my husband wanted to come into the house with me. I was just about to say, "Thanks for a nice time".

Shelley Winters

Women now expect men to watch them have babies. This is called natural childbirth.

Dave Barry

It is said of me that when I was young, I divided my time impartially among wine, women and song. I deny this categorically. Ninety per cent of my interests were women.

Arthur Rubenstein

Between them the two men had a sperm count smaller than Cheltenham Ladies' College.

A.A. Gill

I knew Elizabeth Taylor when she didn't know where her next husband was coming from.

Anne Baxter

I am ninety-five. I still chase girls but I can't remember why.

George Burns

From my experience of life I believe my personal motto should be "Beware of men bearing flowers".

Muriel Spark

My computer dating bureau came up with a perfect gentleman. Still, I've got another three goes.

Sally Poplin

Having a baby is one of the hardest and most strenuous things known to man.

Anna Raeburn

I was married by a judge. I should have asked for a jury.

George Burns

After lovemaking, do you (a) go to sleep? (b) light a cigarette? (c) return to the front of the bus?

Joan Rivers

My wife finds it difficult to envisage me as the end product of millions of years of evolution.

Bob Barnes

Divorce comes from the old Latin word *divorcerum* meaning "having your genitals torn out through your wallet". And the judge said, "All the money and we'll shorten it to alimony."

Robin Williams

There is sex, but it's not what you think. Marvellous for the first fortnight. Then every Wednesday, if there isn't a good late night concert on Radio Three.

Malcolm Bradbury

Woman is a primitive animal who micturates once a day, defecates once a week, menstruates once a month, parturates once a year and copulates whenever she has the opportunity.

Somerset Maugham

When a woman on my show told me she had eighteen children because she loved her husband so much, I told her I loved my cigar too, but I took it out of my mouth once in a while.

Groucho Marx

If he tells you he likes black underwear, stop washing his pants.

Jasmine Birtles

I wouldn't trust my husband with a young woman for five minutes and he's been dead for twenty-five years.

Kathleen Behan

When I fell in love with my wife, I thought those eyes, those lips, those chins. We had to go down the aisle in single file.

Roy Brown

She was looser than an MFI wardrobe.

Roy Brown

The thing that takes up the least amount of time and causes the most trouble is sex

John Barrymore

My wife screams when she is having sex – especially when I walk in on her.

Roy Brown

At whatever stage you apologise to your wife, the answer is always the same – "it's too late now".

Denys Parsons

Women: you can't live with them and you can't get them to dress up in a skimpy Nazi costume and beat you with a warm squash.

Emo Philips

I like my lovers to be female, human and alive, but in a pinch, I'll take any two out of three.

Emo Philips

Love is just a system for getting someone to call you darling after sex.

Julian Barnes

A lot of girls go out with me just to further their careers – damn anthropologists.

Emo Philips

None of us can boast much about the morality of our ancestors: the records do not show that Adam and Eve were married.

Edgar Howe

One of the most difficult things in this world is to convince a woman that even a bargain costs money.

Edgar Howe

If your husband has difficulty in getting to sleep, the words, "We need to talk about our relationship" may help.

Rita Rudner

The worst aspect of marriage is that it makes a woman believe that other men are just as easy to fool.

H. L. Mencken

It isn't premarital sex if you have no intention of getting married.

Matt Barry

A man should marry only a very pretty woman in case he ever wants some other man to take her off his hands.

Sacha Guitry

Men have higher body temperatures than women. If your heating goes out in winter, I recommend sleeping next to a man. Men are basically portable heaters that snore.

Rita Rudner

I'm a great lover, I'll bet.

Emo Philips

I never met a woman that, if you got to know her, didn't want to squeeze your pimples.

David Arnason

Some women think bikinis are immodest, while others have beautiful figures

Olin Miller

Women inspire men to great undertakings and then distract us from carrying them out.

Oscar Wilde

My dog was my only friend. I told my wife that every man needs at least two friends, so she bought me another dog.

Henny Youngman

After a man is married he has the legal right to deceive only one woman.

Edgar Howe

When my jokes are explained to her and she has the leisure to reflect on them, she laughs very heartily.

Sydney Smith

Changeable women are more endurable than monotonous ones; they are sometimes murdered but rarely deserted.

George Bernard Shaw

Few men know how to kiss well – fortunately, I've always had time to teach them.

Mae West

A widower enjoys a second wife as much as a widow enjoys her husband's life insurance.

Edgar Howe

I would like to announce that the notice I put in this newspaper last week was in error. I will be responsible for any debts incurred by my wife. And I will start paying them as soon as I get out of hospital.

Henny Youngman

The penalty for getting the woman is that you must keep her.

Lionel Strachey

Women have a hard enough time in this world – telling them the truth would be too cruel.

H. L. Mencken

Love, Sex, Marriage...

When a man goes crazy, his wife is the first to know it and the last to admit it.

Edgar Howe

A man finds it awfully hard to lie to the woman he loves — the first time.

Helen Rowland

If I ever marry, it will be on a sudden impulse — as a man shoots himself.

H. L. Mencken

When you consider what a chance women have to poison their husbands, it's a wonder there isn't more of it done.

Kin Hubbard

In my day, hot pants were something we had, not wore.

Bette Davis

If you haven't seen your wife smile at a traffic cop, you haven't seen her smile her prettiest.

Kin Hubbard

A woman who takes her husband about with her everywhere is like a cat that goes on playing with a mouse long after she's killed it.

H. H. Munro

An elderly actress I once knew had a claim to fame. She had been seduced by a man with a wooden leg in the Garden of Gethsemane.

Steve Race

I was walking down Soho when a young lady asked if I would sleep with her for fifty dollars. Well, I wasn't tired, but I thought the money would come in handy.

Harry Scott

If you think you're in love just think of him sitting on the lavatory. If you still love him, marry him.

Jean Boht

In the Forties, to get a girl, you had to be a GI or a jock. In the Fifties, to get a girl, you had to be Jewish. In the Sixties, to get a girl, you had to be black. In the Seventies, to get a girl, you have to be a girl.

Mort Sahl

My girlfriend told me I was immature emotionally, sexually and intellectually. I said, 'Yes, but in what other ways?'

Woody Allen

I got married the second time in the same way that when a murder is committed, crackpots turn up at the police station to confess the crime.

Delmore Schwartz

A wedding is a funeral where you smell your own flowers.

Eddie Cantor

I went into a feminist bookstore the other day. I looked more female than anybody in there.

Clint Eastwood

If her dress had pockets my wife would look like a pool table.

Rodney Dangerfield

Lulubelle, it's you! I didn't recognise you standing up.

Groucho Marx

I must marry – if only to get to bed at a reasonable hour.

Benjamin Constant

Marriage is when a woman asks a man to remove his pyjamas because she wants to send them to the laundry.

Albert Finney

A woman told me she would fulfill my ultimate fantasy for £100. I asked her to paint my house.

Sean O'Bryan

Laugh and the world laughs with you. Snore and you sleep alone.

Anthony Burgess

When we were dating we spent most of our time talking about sex – why I couldn't do it, where we could do it, were her parents going to go out so we could do it. Now that we're married, we've got nothing to talk about.

Daniel Stern

My girlfriend has lovely coloured eyes. I particularly like the blue one.

Harry Scott

I wish I had the experience that some woman had killed herself for love of me. The women who have admired me have all insisted on living on, long after I have ceased to care for them.

George Sanders

I've trusted men all my life and I've never been deceived yet – except by my husbands and they don't count.

Mary Boland

I knew I was in love. First of all, I was very nauseous.

Woody Allen

I was incredible in bed last night. I never once had to sit up and consult the manual.

Woody Allen

The charms of a passing woman are usually in direct proportion to the speed of her passing.

Marcel Proust

I've often been chased by women but never while I was awake.

Bob Hope

Media and Films

Marilyn Monroe is good at playing abstract confusion in the same way that a midget is good at being short.

Clive James

Death will be a great relief. No more interviews.

Katharine Hepburn

I got all the schooling any actress needs – I learned to write enough to sign contracts.

Hermione Gingold

Great storytellers, even ones who have been dead for a hundred years, show up extant television writers as semi-literate, unimaginative comatose cliché-mongers.

A. A. Gill

I see my body just as a classy chassis to carry my mind around in.

Sylvester Stallone

I got a letter from Princess Diana thanking me for taking her out of the headlines.

Graham Taylor

When I watched Spencer Tracy playing in Dr. Jekyll and Mr. Hyde I had great difficulty deciding which of them he was portraying at any given moment.

Somerset Maugham

Media and Films

Getting the costumes right in *Cleopatra* was like polishing the fish-knives on the Titanic.

Julian Barnes

The only moving thing about the TV show Neighbours is the scenery.

Victor Lewis-Smith

Reviewers fall into two classes – those who have little to say and those who have nothing.

Max Beerbohm

As in the outfitting of the Titanic, no expense has been spared on this production of *The Romans in Britain*.

Francis King

Diane Keaton's acting style is really a nervous breakdown in slow motion.

John Simon

In writing a western, there has to be woman, but not much of one. A good horse is much more important.

Max Brand

I've played everything except women and midgets.

Robert Mitchum

Once a newspaper touches a story the facts are lost for ever, even to the protagonists.

Norman Mailer

Moi, in the altogether? Honey, no studio has that much money.

Bette Midler

A satire which the censor is able to understand deserves to be banned.

Karl Kraus

The first rule of comedy is never perform in a town where they still point at aeroplanes.

Bobby Mills

If my films make even one more person feel miserable, I'll feel I've done my job.

Woody Allen

I am pleased that television is now showing murder stories because it is bringing murder back into its rightful setting – the home.

Alfred Hitchcock

I've always said there's a place for the press but they haven't dug it yet.

Tommy Docherty

A foreign correspondent is someone who flies around from hotel to hotel and thinks that the most interesting thing about any story is the fact that he has arrived to cover it.

Tom Stoppard

Media and Films

Before I went to see *Deep Throat*, I thought it was a film about a giraffe.

Bob Hope

This film wasn't released – it escaped.

James Caan

Pinter's *The Birthday Party* was like a vintage Hitchcock thriller which has been edited by a cross-eyed studio janitor with a lawnmower.

Orson Welles

Fred Astaire was great, but don't forget that Ginger Rogers did everything that he did, backwards and in high heels.

Bob Thaves

I hesitate to say what the functions of the modern journalist may be, but I imagine that they do not exclude the intelligent anticipation of facts before they occur.

Lord Curzon

Too caustic? To hell with the cost; we'll make the movie anyway.

Samuel Goldwyn

The Chase is the worst thing that has happened to movies since Lassie played a war veteran with amnesia.

Rex Reed

Media and Films

There are three things that are as unfathomable as they are
fascinating to the masculine mind: metaphysics, the feminine
heart and golf.

Alain Haultain

The only thing in my life that I regret is that I once saved
David Frost from drowning.

Peter Cook

Whatever happened to the Elephant Man? He made that
one cracker of a film and that was it.

Jack Dee

I get annoyed at TV programs interrupting the commercials.
I see pretty good acting on the commercials. Anyone who
can get worked up over a bar of soap must be a good actor.

Cedric Hardwicke

TV is a wonderful invention. It lets a person in New York see
someone in Los Angeles suffering from acid indigestion.

Jack Cassidy

Destroy me and you destroy the entire British film industry.

Oliver Reed

My photographs don't do me justice – they look just like
me.

Phyllis Diller

I work for the BBC. I was hoping to go into programme
planning but unfortunately I've got a degree.

John Cleese

If Woody Allen didn't exist then somebody would have knitted him.

Lesley White

Dear Editor, You have asked me to cut three lines from a five thousand word article. I have performed the necessary butchery. Here is the bleeding corpse.

Henry James

Hedda Hopper once came to my table in Chasers when I was having dinner with my husband and said, "What the hell are you doing here? I've got a headline in the papers that you've broken up with Don and are in San Francisco with Glenn Ford. How can you ruin my big exclusive?"

Hope Lange

A reporter is as close to the action as a crablouse to the begetting of a child.

Norman Mailer

I don't want to see the uncut version of ANYTHING.

Jean Kerr

If Bo Derek got the part of Helen Keller she'd have trouble with the dialogue.

Joan Rivers

You had to stand in line to hate Harry Cohn.

Hedda Hopper

How did I get involved in a terrible film like *Best Defence*? The door opened and four men came in carrying a cheque.

Eddie Murphy

The film *Bolero* is intended to be erotic, but it verges on the emetic.

Christopher Tookey

Walt Disney, of course, has the best casting. If he doesn't like an actor he just tears him up.

Alfred Hitchcock

Editing the film *The Boy Friend*, a gorilla in boxing gloves wielding a pair of garden shears could have done a better job.

Ken Russell

This is one of those films that should never have been released, not even on parole.

Christopher Tookey

If I had to do it all over again, I would do exactly the same things, although maybe a little quicker.

James Stewart

Why do I not like Marlon Brando? Because I don't enjoy actors who seek to commune with their armpits.

Greer Garson

The film *Double X* will make money by attracting the kind of audience which stops to watch traffic accidents.

Christopher Tookey

They say Tom Mix rides as if he's part of the horse, but they don't say which part.

Robert Sherwood

You cannot hope to bribe or twist, thank God, the British journalist, but seeing what the man will do unbribed, there's no occasion to.

Humbert Wolfe

My seventh film, *The Cool Mikado*, had the appearance of being made in a wind tunnel.

Frankie Howerd

There are basically only two types of exercise in Hollywood: jogging and helping a recently divorced friend move.

Robert Wagner

I would praise Joad's new book, but modesty forbids.

Bertrand Russell

Sitting through this movie is like having someone at a fancy Parisian restaurant who neither speaks nor reads French, read out stentoriously the entire long menu in his best Arkansas accent and occasionally interrupt himself to chortle at his cleverness.

John Simon

In the seventies I worked on an alternative magazine called *What's on in Stoke Newington*. It was just a sheet of paper with bugger all written on it.

Alexei Sayle

Imitation is the sincerest form of television.

Fred Allen

Never under any circumstances write comedy for laughs.
This is as ruinous as believing that your wife means it when
she says, "Tell me all about her. I swear I don't mind."

Hugh Leonard

Never judge a book by its movie.

J. W. Eagan

Peter Sellers had a total of four wives and eight heart attacks.

John Frank-Keyes

This is the operator. Am I speaking to the party to whom I
am connected?

Lily Tomlin

The importance of a public speaker bears an inverse
relationship to the number of microphones into which he
speaks.

William Morgan

Always pass over the newspaper at the top of the pile because
the ones underneath have better and fresher news.

Mike Sharp

It's a rule that TV brides must be plain at a pinch and
grotesque at best. This adds an extra squeeze of syrupy
sentiment to the wedding. Ah, you say, there really is
something for everyone.

A. A. Gill

My father hated radio and could not wait for television to be invented so he could hate that too.

Peter De Vries

Radio and television sure are funny – all except the comedy programs.

Fred Allen

A great editor is a man of outstanding talent who owns 51 per cent of his newspaper's stock.

Henry Watterson

The critics were very kind to our film. It was word of mouth that killed it.

Arthur Askey

We should be eternally grateful to the person who invented the idiot box on the envelope that tells a person where to place the stamp when they can't quite figure it out for themselves.

Karen O'Byrne

Many a good newspaper story has been ruined by oververification.

James Bennett

The trouble with photographing beautiful women is that you'll never get into the dark room until after they've gone.

Yussef Karsh

An apostrophe is used mainly in hand-lettered small business signs to alert the reader that an "s" is coming up at the end of the word.

Dave Barry

I love deadlines. I like the whooshing sound they make as they fly by.

Douglas Adams

Journalism consists in buying white paper at two cents a pound and selling it at ten cents a pound.

Charles Dana

Grampian Television was originally going to be called Scottish Highlands and Islands Television – until someone pointed out that the initials would not be entirely appropriate or perhaps too appropriate.

Russell Ash

The worst thing that could happen on my show is that somebody might learn something.

Dave Letterman

Madonna has just lost thirty pounds – she shaved her legs.

Joan Rivers

A journalist has no ideas and the ability to express them.

Karl Kraus

I apologise for the lack of bloodshed on tonight's programme. We shall try to do better next time.

Alfred Hitchcock

Television is chewing gum for the mind.

Frank Lloyd Wright

Women reporters who ask awkward questions are just trying to prove their manhood.

Ross Perot

Terry Wogan is so versatile; he can talk a load of old blarney on television and on radio.

Caroline Hook

The scene is too dull. Tell him to put more life into his dying.

Sam Goldwyn

Give me a smart idiot before a stupid genius any day.

Sam Goldwyn

Helping with the casting, I had my first look at Cary Grant and I said "If he can talk, I'll take him."

Mae West

Elizabeth Taylor has grown so ample that it has become necessary to dress her almost exclusively in a variety of ambulatory tents. On the few occasions when she does reveal her bosom (or part thereof), one breast (or part thereof) proves sufficient to traverse an entire wide-screen frame – diagonally.

John Simon

Audrey Hepburn is a walking x-ray.

Billy Wilder

My ambition is to host a TV chat show with Neil Armstrong as a guest and never once mention the moon.

Ardal O'Hanlon

Over in Hollywood they almost made a great picture, but they caught it in time.

Wilson Mizner

Medicine and Doctors

Medicine and Doctors

Psychiatry's chief contribution to philosophy is the discovery that the toilet is the seat of the soul.

Alexander Chase

One of the minor pleasures in life is to be slightly ill.

Harold Nicolson

Insect repellent is one of a number of joke items available in any chemist shop.

Henry Beard

You go to a psychiatrist when you're slightly cracked and keep going until you're completely broke.

Joan Rivers

I had a video made of my recent knee operation. The doctor said it was the best movie I ever starred in.

Shirley MacLaine

I've just had an operation for piles – all my troubles are behind me.

Ken Brett

Humans can survive easily without an appendix, but surgeons can do so only with difficulty.

Rudolf Virchow

My doctor has always told me to smoke. He even explains himself: Smoke, my friend. Otherwise someone will smoke in your place.

Erik Satie

Medicine and Doctors

A doctor is the only man without a guaranteed cure for a cold.

Dominic Cleary

He is so fat he hasn't seen his privates in twenty years.

Carson McCullers

It is amazing what little harm doctors do when one considers all the opportunities they have.

Mark Twain

Just once I'd like to see the win-loss records of doctors right out front where people could see them – won ten, lost three, tied two.

Abe Lemons

I'm at the age where my back goes out more than I do.

Phyllis Diller

Sometimes I think I give and care too much. In fact my gynaecologist looked up the other day and said "Dame Edna, when will you ever stop giving?"

Edna Everage

Lady Bullock, who had been at death's door for so long now that one might have been pardoned for mistaking her for its knocker.

Leon Garfield

Medicine and Doctors

Anyone who gives a surgeon six thousand dollars for breast augmentation should give some thought to investing a little more in brain augmentation.

Mike Royko

I don't jog because when I die I want to be sick.

Abe Lemons

Shh, don't wake him up! He's got a bad case of insomnia and he's trying to sleep it off.

Chico Marx

After twelve years of therapy, my psychiatrist said something that brought tears to my eyes. He said "No hablo ingles".

Ronnie Shakes

A psychiatrist is the next man you start talking to after you start talking to yourself.

Fred Allen

A neurotic is a person who builds a castle in the air. A psychotic is the person who lives in it. A psychiatrist is the person who collects the rent.

Jerome Lawrence

If I am ever stuck on a respirator or a life support system, I definitely want to be unplugged, but not until I get down to a size eight.

Henriette Mantel

Medicine and Doctors

My doctor recently told me that jogging would add years to my life. I think he was right. I feel ten years older already.

Milton Berle

Minor surgery is what other people have.

Bill Watson

My parents enjoyed good health. In fact they loved it.

Gracie Allen

If you've got water on the knee, you're not aiming straight.

Tim Denes

If I put on five more pounds I will be eligible for statehood.

Audrey Buslik

I am anorexic actually. Anorexic people look in the mirror and think they look fat, and so do I.

Jo Brand

He's a schizophrenic with low self esteem. He thinks he's one person.

Bill Schorr

I've got a friend who's a procrastinator – he didn't get a birthmark until he was eight years old.

Steven Wright

Medicine and Doctors

I was in analysis. I was suicidal. I would have killed myself but my analyst was a strict Freudian and if you kill yourself they make you pay for the sessions you miss.

Woody Allen

Medicine is basically the study of various liquids and solids that – either naturally or by force – go into and come out of the human body.

Ryan Anthony

The average human being has one breast and one testicle.

Stephen Grollman

When I was little I had to beg a boy to play doctors with me. He finally agreed, but he sent me a bill.

Joan Rivers

Nine out of ten doctors agree that one out of ten doctors is an idiot.

Jay Leno

It is truly written that a man has five times as many fingers as ears, but only twice as many ears as noses.

Don Geddis

I didn't sleep well. I made several mistakes.

Steven Wright

It was a non-smoker who committed the first sin and brought death into the world and all our woe.

Robert Lynd

There are three kinds of death in this world. There's heart death, there's brain death and there's being off the network.

Guy Almes

I love all you ex-smokers – because you leave more cigarettes for me.

Denis Leary

Sometimes a cigar is just a cigar.

Sigmund Freud

Having smoking and non smoking sections in the same room is like having urinating and non-urinating sections in a swimming pool.

Ross Parker

Do you know what doctors call teenage motorcyclists? Organ donors.

Patrick Murray

After two days in hospital, I took a turn for the nurse.

W. C. Fields

Lord, grant patience (sic) to our doctors.

Patrick Murray

Medicine and Doctors

A doctor's reputation is made by the number of eminent men who die under his care.

George Bernard Shaw

I was once thrown out of a mental hospital for depressing the other patients.

Oscar Levant

Mrs. Harvey, the stitches will come out in seven or eight days so there is no reason why in about two weeks you cannot begin denying your husband sex again.

Mark Bryant

With friends like you, who needs enemas?

Matthew Broderick

Be careful about reading health books. You may die of a misprint.

Mark Twain

Music

 **Music**

The notes I handle no better than many pianists. But the pauses between the notes – ah, that is where the art resides.

Artur Schnabel

If one hears bad music, it is one's duty to drown it out by one's conversation.

Oscar Wilde

I go back to Bach as a sick dog instinctively grubs at the roots and herbs that are its right medicine.

Pablo Casals

The harpsichord is a performance on a bird-cage with a toasting fork.

Percy A. Scholes

Elgar's first symphony is the musical equivalent of St. Pancras Railway Station.

Thomas Beecham

You can tell how bad a musical is by the number of times the chorus yells "hooray".

John Crosby

Musical comedy is the Irish stew of drama. Anything may be put into it with the certainty that it will improve the general effect.

P. G. Wodehouse

The best instrument is the bag-pipes. They sound exactly the same when you have finished learning them as when you start.

Thomas Beecham

There are three kinds of pianists: Jewish pianists, homosexual pianists and bad pianists.

Vladimir Horowitz

The music performed at amateur concerts seemed to have been designed to make those who play it happy and drive those who listen to despair.

Adolphe Adam

Thomas Beecham was a pompous little band-master who stood against everything creative in the art of his time.

John Fowles

She was a singer who had to take every note above A with her eyebrows.

Montague Glass

Disc-jockeys are electronic lice.

Anthony Burgess

There are just two golden rules for an orchestra – start together and finish together. The public doesn't give a damn what goes on in between.

Thomas Beecham

Faure writes the sort of music a pederast might hum when raping a choirboy.

Marcel Proust

Music helps set a romantic mood. Imagine her surprise when you say "We don't need a stereo – I have an accordion".

Martin Mull

Rossini addressed his letters to his mother as "mother of the famous composer".

Robert Browning

If I had my life to live over again, I should devote it to the arrangement of headphones and microphones or the like whereby the noises used by musical maniacs should be audible to themselves only. It should be made a felony to play a musical instrument in any other than a completely soundproof room.

George Bernard Shaw

It has been said that if the opening phrase of a classical minuet can be fitted to the words "Are you the O'Reilly who owns this hotel?" then it was written by Haydn; if it can't then it wasn't.

Gervase Hughes

The tuba is certainly the most intestinal of instruments, the very lower bowel of music.

Peter de Vries

Anton Bruckner wrote the same symphony nine times (ten, actually) trying to get it right. He failed.

Edward Abbey

Dame Kiri Te Kanawa is a viable alternative to valium.

Ira Siff

My advice to all who want to attend a lecture on music is "Don't"; go to a concert instead.

Ralph Vaughan-Williams

Ladies of the choir, I want you to sound like twenty-two women having babies without chloroform.

John Barbirolli

Going to the opera, like getting drunk, is a sin that carries its own punishment with it.

Hannah More

When Jack Benny plays the violin, it sounds as though the strings are still in the cat.

Fred Allen

Beethoven always sounds to me like the upsetting of a bag of nails, with here and there also a dropped hammer.

John Ruskin

The secret of my piano playing is that I always make sure that the lid over the keyboard is open before I start to play.

Artur Schnabel

I'm in a class by myself, along with people like Rod Stewart.
Engelbert Humperdinck

An unalterable and unquestioned law of the musical world requires that the German text of French operas sung by Swedish artists should be translated into Italian for the clearer understanding of English speaking audiences.
Edith Wharton

During this terzetto, the Reverend Mr. Portpipe fell asleep and accompanied the performance with rather a deeper bass than was generally deemed harmonious.
Thomas L. Peacock

I have been going to symphony concerts for over fifty years, and I find I mind it less and less.
Louise Kent

Madam, you ask me how I compose. I compose sitting down.
Tchaikovsky

The closest sound to Roseanne Barr's singing the National Anthem was my cat being neutered.
Johnny Carson

Troubadours travelled from town to town. They didn't really sing too good, which is the main reason they kept going.
Art Linkletter

The music of Wagner imposes mental tortures that only algebra has the right to inflict.

Paul de Saint-Victor

Modern music is three farts and a raspberry, orchestrated.

John Barbirolli

Riegger's *Dichotomy* sounded as though a pack of rats were being slowly tortured to death, while, from time to time a dying cow moaned.

Walter Abendroth

I would have given my right arm to have been a pianist.

Bobby Robson

Music hath charms to soothe a savage beast – but I'd try a revolver first.

Josh Billings

Nothing soothes me more after a long and maddening course of piano recitals than to sit and have my teeth drilled.

George Bernard Shaw

I do not mind what language an opera is sung in as long as I do not understand it.

Edward Appleton

 **Music**

If you can imagine a man having a vasectomy without anaesthetic to the sound of frantic sitar playing, you will have some idea of what popular Turkish music is like.

Bill Bryson

One good thing about playing a piece of modern music is that if you make a mistake, no one notices.

Gordon Brown

When Brahms is in extra good spirits, he sings, "The grave is my joy".

Tchaikovsky

Liszt's so-called piano music is nothing but Chopin and brandy.

James Huneker

I wonder if George Gershwin had to do it all over again, would he fall in love with himself again?

Oscar Levant

I like Wagner's music better than anybody's. It is so loud that one can talk the whole time without other people hearing what one says.

Oscar Wilde

Schubert sweated beauty as naturally as a Christian sweats hate.

H. L. Mencken

I think Mick Jagger would be astounded and amazed if he realised how many people do not regard him as a sex symbol.

Angie Bowie

Jim Morrison is dead now and that's a high price to pay for immortality.

Gloria Estefan

I think a lot of Leonard Bernstein – but not as much as he does.

Oscar Levant

My orchestra are just assassins.

Arturo Toscanini

If Beethoven had been killed in a plane crash, it would have changed the history of music and of aviation.

Tom Stoppard

The Pogues have done for Irish music what Shane McGowan did for dentistry.

Roy Gullane

Too many pieces of music finish too long after the end.

Igor Stravinsky

There's nothing remarkable about it. All one has to do is to hit the right keys at the right time and the instrument plays itself.

Johann Sebastian Bach

The world we live in is in a funny state. Someone goes out and shoots John Lennon and lets Des O'Connor live.

Roy Brown

The music critic, Huneber, could never quite make up his mind about a new symphony until he had seen the composer's mistress.

H. L. Mencken

The trouble with opera is that there is always too much singing.

Claude Debussy

The trouble with a lot of songs you hear nowadays is that somebody forgot to put them to music.

Sammy Kahn

The chief objection to playing wind instruments is that it prolongs the life of the player beyond all reasonable limits.

George Bernard Shaw

After conducting a concert in a small town, I once received the following note from a farmer who had attended the performance: "Dear Sir, I wish to inform you that the man who played the long thing you pull in and out only did so during the brief periods you were looking at him."

Arturo Toscanini

With regard to Gounod's *Redemption*, if you will only take the precaution to go in long enough after it commences and to come out long enough before it is over, you will not find it wearisome.

George Bernard Shaw

People who have heard me sing say I don't.

Mark Twain

Let a short Act of Parliament be passed, placing all street musicians outside the protection of the law, so that any citizen may assail them with stones, sticks, knives, pistols or bombs without incurring any penalties.

George Bernard Shaw

Nationalities and Places

The Americans, who are the most efficient people on earth, have invented so wide a range of pithy and hackneyed phrases that they can carry on a conversation without giving a moment's reflection to what they are actually saying and so leave their minds free to consider the more important matters of big business and fornication.

Somerset Maugham

The IRA are indiscriminately killing men, women and children and now they have killed two Australians.

Margaret Thatcher

I can never forgive God for having created the French.

Peter Ustinov

The Russians have never put a man on the moon. They are afraid he might defect.

Kenneth Robertson

You are not a proper member of an Irish club until you become barred.

Michael Davitt

The fact remains that the common speech of the Commonwealth of Australia represents the most brutal maltreatment which has ever been inflicted upon the mother-tongue of the great English-speaking nations.

William Churchill

Patriotism is the conviction that your country is superior to all others because you were born in it.

George Bernard Shaw

I have an important message for the American people –
always place the shower curtain on the inside of the bath.

Conrad Hilton

We British may not be the greatest at winning the Winter
Olympics, but at least we carry our bloody flag properly.

Mike Freeman

An Englishman's real ambition is to get a railway
compartment to himself.

Ian Hay

How can what an Englishman believes be heresy? It is a
contradiction in terms.

George Bernard Shaw

This type of thing may be tolerated by the French, but we
are British, thank God.

Bernard Montgomery

We should give the Somalis better arms and better military
training and then seal the borders.

P. J. O'Rourke

In Alaska, we have just two seasons – this winter and next
winter.

Leigh Wade

Show a Welshman 1001 exits and he will go through the one
marked "Self-destruction".

Richard Burton

I must be the luckiest man in the world. Not only am I bisexual, I am also Welsh.

John Osborne

God created alcohol just to stop the Irish from ruling the world.

Patrick Murray

German is a language which was developed solely to afford the speaker the opportunity to spit at strangers under the guise of polite conversation.

P. J. O'Rourke

The broad Australian accent is not a lovesome thing, I grant you. At its worst, it is reminiscent of a dehydrated crow uttering its last statement on life from the bough of a dead tree in the middle of a clay-pan at the peak of a seven-year drought.

Buzz Kennedy

Realising that they will never be a world power, the Cypriots have decided to settle for being a world nuisance.

George Mikes

The typical West of Ireland family consists of father, mother, twelve children and resident Dutch anthropologist.

Flann O'Brien

American politicians will do anything for money; English politicians take the money and won't do anything.

Stephen Leacock

Nationalities and Places

In Scotland we have a verdict "not proven". That means "not guilty, but don't do it again".

Andrew Brodie

The national dish of America is menus.

Robert Robinson

There is nothing wrong with California that the San Andreas fault cannot cure.

Ross McDonald

Poms don't have much imagination because they have pinched most of their street names off the monopoly board.

Paul Hogan

Bolivians are barely metamorphosed llamas, who have learned to talk but not to think.

Jose Merino

The opponents in the American Civil War are cutting each others' throats because one half of them prefer hiring their servants for life and the other for the hour.

Thomas Carlyle

The national sport of England is obstacle racing. People fill their rooms with useless and cumbersome furniture and spend the rest of their lives in trying to dodge it.

Herbert Tree

There are only two classes of person in New South Wales – those who have been convicted and those who ought to have been.

Lachlan MacQuarie

The people of Crete unfortunately make more history than they can consume locally.

Andrei Sakharov

The only pleasure an Englishman has is in passing on his cold germs.

Gerald Durrell

I have just returned from Boston. It's the only thing to do if you find yourself there.

Fred Allen

The English are a race of cold-blooded queers with nasty complexions and terrible teeth who once conquered half the world but still haven't figured out central heating. They warm their beers and chill their baths and boil all their food, including bread.

P.J. O'Rourke

When Mel Brooks told his mother that he was marrying an Italian girl, she said "Bring her over. I'll be in the kitchen – with my head in the oven."

Anne Bancroft

The kids from fifteen countries took math and science tests. The U.S.A. came fourteenth, behind Slovenia, which has been a country only since last Tuesday.

Bill Maher

The motto for Cleveland is "You gotta live somewhere".
Jimmy Brogan

Given the unlikely options of attending a funeral or a sex orgy, a true Irishman will always opt for the funeral.
John B. Keane

There is no housing shortage in England today. That's just a rumour put about by people who have nowhere to live.
G. L. Murfin

The East German manages to combine a teutonic capacity for bureaucracy with a Russian capacity for infinite delay.
Goronwy Rees

Here's to the harp of old Ireland and may it never want for a string as long as there's a gut in a peeler.
Brendan Behan

In England it is considered good to kill an admiral from time to time, to encourage the others.
Voltaire

The reason why the Australian accent can be offensive to the ear is flies. Australians speak as if there were a tax on lip movement because to open their mouth further would be to allow in flies.
James Oram

I don't feel we did wrong in taking this great country away from them. There were great numbers of people who needed new land and the Indians were selfishly trying to keep it for themselves.

John Wayne

From every Englishman there emanates a kind of gas, the deadly choke-damp of boredom.

Heinrich Heine

A complete description of Belfast is given by: population 200,000; early closing day Wednesday.

Shamus O'Shamus

Just arrived in Venice. Streets full of water. Please advise.

Robert Benchley

I really hate America – we've turned into such selfish bastards. If Adolf Hitler came back and said "I will reduce taxes" he'd win by a landslide.

Peter Buck

British ferries have stopped carrying live animals to the Continent. This is making it very difficult for English fans to get to away matches.

Jo Brand

The Soviet bureaucracy is about as efficient as a Mexican traffic court that doesn't take bribes.

Whitney Brown

Nationalities and Places

Australia is the only country in the world where the word "academic" is regularly used as a term of abuse.

Leonie Kramer

American toilet paper is so thin that you have to use three sheets and the beer tastes like weasel piss.

Joe Jackson

Living in provincial England is like being married to a stupid but exquisitely beautiful wife.

Margaret Halsey

Of course I don't mind the fight being at three in the morning. Everyone in Glasgow fights at three in the morning.

Jim Watt

The European Community is being run in a thoroughly un-British way.

Lord Bethell

The devil take the English and their language! They take a dozen monosyllabic words in their jaws, chew them crunch them and spit them out again and call that speaking.

Heinrich Heine

He had an alibi tighter than a Scotch auditor.

Marco Page

The Japanese have perfected good manners and made them indistinguishable from rudeness.

Paul Theroux

The Americans don't really understand what is going on in Bosnia. To them, it's the unspellables killing the unpronouncables.

P. J. O'Rourke

An Irish queer is a fellow who prefers women to drink.

Sean O'Faolain

Where I come from, the valleys are so narrow the dogs have to wag their tails up and down.

Sam Snead

A nation is a society united by a delusion about its ancestry and by a common hatred of its neighbours.

William R. Inge

France is a country where the money falls apart in your hands and you cannot tear the toilet paper.

Billy Wilder

Australians are basically a bunch of sexist loud-mouth drunks, but I once met a group near Wagga-Wagga in the Northern Territories who were the complete opposite. Not only were they quiet and reserved, but they also happened to be vegetarian teetotallers. However, before I had a chance to speak to them, they hopped away into the bush.

Kelvin Birdseye

In France, quarrels strengthen a love affair; in America they end it.

Ned Rorem

Nationalities and Places

Nationalism means that every little group of human twerps with its own slang, haircut and pet name for God should have a country.

P. J. O'Rourke

Never shoot a film in Belgrade, Yugoslavia. The whole town is illuminated by a twenty-watt night-light and there's nothing to do. You can't even go for a drive. Tito is always using the car.

Mel Brooks

If you want to do something for the dignity of the people in the sub-Saharan countries, you can stop donating bell-bottom pants to Goodwill.

P. J. O'Rourke

The Americans are a funny lot. They drink whiskey to keep them warm, then they put ice in it to make it cool; then they put some sugar in it to make it sweet and then they put a slice of lemon in it to make it sour. Then they say, "Here's to you" and drink it themselves.

B. N. Chakravarty

The broad Australian accent is a legitimate form of speech and should not be stigmatized as a speech defect needing correction.

John Ingram

One Parisian night will adjust my losses on the battlefield.

Napoleon Bonaparte

Places like Norwich make me want to get a machine gun and kill everybody.

Carole Morin

Mundane constraints of space and time do not apply to stories about Oxford.

Robert May

Why cannot people learn to speak the truth? I have, I think, taught two, perhaps three, Indian colleagues to do so. It will probably wreck their careers.

J. B. S. Haldane

I never deal with countries who have green in their flag or where people do not wear overcoats in winter.

Benjamin Slade

I once heard a Californian student in Heidelberg say, in one of his calmest moods that he would rather decline two drinks than one German adjective.

Mark Twain

I asked a Burmese man why women, after centuries of following their men, now walk ahead. He said there were many unexploded landmines since the war.

Robert Mueller

If the mountains of Switzerland were knocked down and thrown into the lakes, two problems could be solved at once.

Lord Curzon

The sooner the Welsh language disappears the better.

Matthew Arnold

Nationalities and Places

My entire involvement with the Irish Literary Revival consisted in standing beside Mister W. B. Yeats in the urinal during an interval at the Abbey Theatre, where I remember he was having great difficulty with his waterworks.

Eoin O'Mahony

The French don't care what they do as long as they pronounce it properly.

George Bernard Shaw

The Welsh are just Italians in the rain.

Nancy Banks-Smith

A bomb under the West car park at Twickenham on an international day would end fascism in England for a generation.

Philip Toynbee

In America policemen shout "Stop or I'll shoot, bang bang". In Los Angeles policemen shout "bang bang, stop or I'll shoot". In England policemen shout "Stop or I'll shout stop again".

Robin Williams

If it were not necessary to eat or wear clothes, Russia would be the greatest country in the world.

Yakov Smirnoff

There is nothing the British like more than a bloke who comes from nowhere, makes it and then gets clobbered.

Melvyn Bragg

The pretty girls in Utah mostly marry Young.

Artemus Ward

The English think of an opinion as something which a decent person, if he has the misfortune to have one, does all he can to hide.

Margaret Halsey

Mistresses are common in California – in fact some of them are very common. It's easier for a man to conceal his mistress there because of the smog.

Groucho Marx

The English hate children. They keep their dogs at home and send their kids off to high class kennels, called Eton and Harrow.

Kathy Lette

The trouble with these international events is that they attract foreigners.

Robert Morley

They say that if the Swiss had designed the Alps, they would be rather flatter.

Paul Theroux

The best tribute a French translator can pay Shakespeare is
not to translate him.

Max Beerbohm

The fantasy of every Australian woman is to have two men –
one cleaning and one dusting.

Maureen Murphy

Anyone who has been educated in an English public school
and served in the ranks of the British army is quite at home
in a Third World prison.

Roger Cooper

The more underdeveloped the country, the more
overdeveloped the women.

J. K. Galbraith

Everything German is odious to me. The German language
rends my ears. At times my own poems nauseate me when I
see they are written in German.

Heinrich Heine

Devilishly clever race the French. How they speak that
unspeakable language of theirs defeats me.

Leslie Howard

If you speak three languages, you are trilingual. If you speak
two languages, you're bilingual. If you speak one language,
you're American.

Sonny Spoon

I look upon Scotland as an inferior sort of Switzerland.

Sydney Smith

The Roman Empire declined and fell because it takes all day to say anything in Latin. If your house is on fire or Attila the Hun is at the gate and you've gotta stop and think of tenses, cases and conjugations before you can call for help, brother, you're dead.

Dobie Gillis

Russ Parker was described as having a couple of kangaroos loose in the back paddock.

Barry Humphreys

Britain has football hooligans, Germany has neo-Nazis and France has farmers.

Bernard Levin

Hating soccer is more American than apple pie.

Tom Weir

My watch is three hours fast and I can't fix it. So I'm going to move to New York.

Steven Wright

The English, who now feel inferior to almost every nation on earth, at least have the Welsh to look down on.

Jan Morris

The ancient Phoenicians believed that the sun was carried across the sky on the back of an enormous snake. So what? So they were idiots.

Dave Barry

Australians are living proof that aborigines screw kangaroos.

John Freeman

Canadians are generally indistinguishable from Americans and the surest way of telling the two apart is to make this observation to a Canadian.

Richard Starnes

Murphy did the 100 meters in record time. He got six months – they were gas meters.

Frank Carson

America is a society which believes that God is dead but Elvis is alive.

Irving Kupcinet

When I told the people of Northern Ireland that I was an atheist, a woman in the audience stood up and asked if it was the Catholic God or the Protestant God I didn't believe in.

Quentin Crisp

I love California – I practically grew up in Phoenix.

Dan Quayle

Dublin was a clear winner in the Irish Tourist Board's "Dirty Towns" competition. The strong smell of the Liffey with its fascinating tang of urine, excreta, rotten dogs and decayed fish sent Dublin into the unassailable lead.

Donal Foley

When St. Patrick first visited Ireland there was no word in the Irish language to express sobriety.

Oliver St. John Gogarty

English is the perfect language to sell pigs in.

Michael Hartnett

Anyone who isn't confused in Northern Ireland doesn't really know what is going on.

John Hume

I have just returned from a trip to Paris and let me tell you lads, that sex in Ireland is only in its infancy.

Patrick Kavanagh

Chicago is a city where men are men and the police take VISA.

Hugh Leonard

In India, "cold weather" is merely a conventional phrase and has come into use through the necessity of having some way to distinguish between weather which will melt a brass door knob and weather which only makes it mushy.

Mark Twain

They drive so crazily in Chicago that anything moving slower than 65 mph is considered to be a house.

J. Joshua

I went to join the New York Public Library. The guy told me I would have to prove I was a citizen of New York, so I stabbed him.

Emo Philips

Of course, if one had enough money to go to America, one wouldn't go.

Oscar Wilde

Almost invariably, fugitive criminals, within a comparatively short space of time, return to England. They cannot live without the smell of drains, fish and chips and the taste of Watneys beer.

James Saunders

An Irish farmer, to cover the possibility of unexpected visitors, can often be found eating his dinner out of a drawer.

Niall Toibin

No matter how great your triumphs or how tragic your defeats remember that approximately one billion Chinese people couldn't care less.

Abraham Lazlo

Outside of the killings, Washington has one of the lowest crime rates in the country.

Marion Barry

Nationalities and Places

Americans adore me and will go on adoring me until I say
something nice about them.

George Bernard Shaw

Illegal aliens have always been a problem in the United
States. Ask any Indian.

Robert Orben

The English should give Ireland Home Rule and reserve the
motion picture rights.

Will Rogers

Americans are a broad-minded people. They will accept the
fact that a person can be an alcoholic, a dope fiend, a wife
beater and even a newspaperman, but if a man doesn't drive,
there's something wrong with him.

Art Buchwald

If I wanted to start an insane asylum, I would just admit
applicants that thought they knew something about Russia.

Will Rogers

You cannot underestimate the intelligence of the American
people.

H. L. Mencken

France is a relatively small and eternally quarrelsome country
in Western Europe, the fountainhead of rationalist political
maniacs, militarily impotent, historically inglorious during
the past century, democratically bankrupt, Communist-
infiltrated from top to bottom.

William F. Buckley

Personally, I prefer to be called a "person of paleness" if you must refer to my "race".

Dan Henry

When a Roman was returning from a trip, he used to send someone ahead to let his wife know, so as not to surprise her in the act.

Montaigne

In the German language, the fish is a he, the scales are she and the fishwife it.

Mark Twain

China actually has the greatest number of speakers of the English language of any country in the world. The trouble is, nobody can understand any of them

Julian Bond

The streets are safe in Philadelphia. It's only the people who make them unsafe.

Frank Rizzo

I showed my appreciation of my native land in the usual way by getting out of it as soon as I possibly could.

George Bernard Shaw

Afrikaans sounds like Welsh with attitude and emphysema.

A. A. Gill

God is good to the Irish, but no one else is, not even the Irish.

Austin O'Malley

Edmonton isn't exactly the end of tEdworld, but you can see it from there.

Ralph Klein

Belgium is a country invented by the British to annoy the French.

Charles De Gaulle

America is a mistake, a giant mistake.

Sigmund Freud

Los Angeles is the plastic asshole of the world.

William Faulkner

America is the only country in the world where failing to promote yourself is regarded as being arrogant.

Garry Trudeau

A nuclear fallout shelter in Barnsley has been damaged by vandals.

Steve Race

An asylum for the sane would be empty in America.

George Bernard Shaw

People say New Yorkers can't get along. Not true. I saw two New Yorkers, complete strangers, sharing a cab. One guy took the tyres and the radio; the other guy took the engine.

David Letterman

New York is the only city in the world where you can get deliberately run over on the sidewalk by a pedestrian.

Russell Baker

My first qualification for mayor of the City of New York is my monumental ingratitude to all of you.

Fiorello LaGuardia

Politics

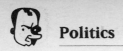

I looked into Dan Quayle's blue eyes and I might as well have been looking out the window.

William Cnaugh

Now that democracy is replacing communism in Eastern Europe, it means the end of elections that are rigged – and the beginning of elections that are bought.

Joe Hickman

My opponent can compress the most words into the fewest ideas of anyone I've ever known.

Abraham Lincoln

Politics is the conduct of public affairs for private advantage.

Ambrose Bierce

An international political alliance is the union of two thieves who have their hands so deeply inserted in each other's pocket that they cannot separately plunder a third.

Ambrose Bierce

Politicians are two notches below child-molesters on the social scale.

John Brown

Mario Cuomo is like Al Capone, but without the charm.

Taki

Einstein's theory of relativity, as practised by Congressmen, simply means getting as many of your family as possible on the pay-roll.

James H. Brown

I fired Douglas MacArthur because he wouldn't respect the office of the president. I didn't fire him because he was a dumb son of a bitch, although he was.

Harry S. Truman

A parliament elected by the universal suffrage of voters grouped according to geographical areas, is about as truly representative as a bottle of Bovril is a true representation of an ox.

Eleanor Rathbone

There are two problems in my life. The political ones are insoluble and the economic ones are incomprehensible.

Alec Douglas-Home

The longer Ferdinand is dead, the more perfect he becomes in my mind.

Imelda Marcos

The fact is, although adultery may be acceptable to the Tory party, buggery certainly isn't.

Tim Renton

The two most powerful men in Russia were Tsar Nicholas II and the last man who spoke to him.

A. J. P. Taylor

John Major is not a man to go tiger shooting with.

Paul Johnson

Tory is a term derived from an Irish word meaning "savage".

Samuel Johnson

The War Office kept three sets of figures: one to mislead the public, another to mislead the Cabinet and a third to mislead itself.

Herbert Asquith

The Ku Klux Klan. They wear white sheets and their hats have a point – which is more than can be said for their beliefs.

Robert Frost

The House of Lords is an ermine-lined dustbin, an upmarket geriatric home with a faint smell of urine.

Austin Mitchell

If Kitchener was not a great man, he was at least a great poster.

Margot Asquith

We in the Republican party have never said that Clinton is a philandering, pot-smoking draft-dodger.

Mary Matalin

Dan Quayle looks like Robert Redford's retarded brother that they kept up in the attic, and he got out somehow.

Patti Marx

Politicians are people who, when they see the light at the end of the tunnel, order more tunnel.

John Quintan

There is nothing more disgusting in British political life than a Conservative who thinks he has public opinion behind him.

Auberon Waugh

The flood is the worst disaster in California since I was elected.

Pat Brown

Only General Burnside could snatch a spectacular defeat out of the jaws of victory.

Abraham Lincoln

It is not enough to have every intelligent person in the country voting for me. I need a majority.

Adlai Stevenson

The honourable member's speech reminds me of Columbus. When he set out, he didn't know where he was going, when he got there he didn't know where he was and when he returned home he didn't know where he'd been.

Winston Churchill

I would not put Jimmy Carter in charge of snake control in Ireland.

Eugene McCarthy

Theodore Roosevelt was an old maid with testosterone poisoning.

Patricia O'Toole

John Major delivers all his statements as though auditioning for the speaking clock.

Stephen Glover

I have one consolation after a life-time in politics. No candidate was ever elected ex-president by such a large majority.

William Taft

Vote for the man who promises least; he'll be the least disappointing.

Bernard Baruch

I cannot bring myself to speak to a woman who has been voice- trained to speak to me as though my dog has just died.

Keith Waterhouse

Oh, if I could only piss the way David Lloyd George speaks.

George Clemenceau

A Conservative is a statesman who is enamoured of existing evils, as distinguished from a Liberal, who wishes to replace them with others.

Ambrose Bierce

A politician will always be there when he needs you.

Ian Walsh

If we don't succeed, we run the risk of failure.

Dan Quayle

Washington couldn't tell a lie, Nixon couldn't tell the truth and Reagan couldn't tell the difference.

Mort Sahl

I have not heard from the Ambassador to Spain for over two years. If I do not hear from him in the next year, I intend to write him a letter.

Thomas Jefferson

Elections are held to delude the populace into believing that they are participating in government.

Gerald Lieberman

The best description of Margaret Thatcher I ever heard is that she's just the sort of woman who wouldn't give you your ball back.

Mike Harding

The only reason I'm not running for president is I'm afraid no woman will come forward and say she's slept with me.

Garry Shandling

The typical British MP stands for election, sits in the House and lies just about all the time.

Winston Churchill

It never occurred to Stalin that the British electorate would remove Churchill from office in the very moment of victory. The result not only surprised but startled him, confirming his rooted belief that elections where the outcome was not guaranteed were too dangerous to be allowed.

Alan Bullock

When Stalin says "dance", a wise man dances.

Nikita Khrushchev

The Right Honourable gentleman has sat so long on the fence that the iron has entered his soul.

David Lloyd-George

If Stalin had learned to play cricket, the world would now be a better place to live in.

Robert Downey

George Bush's problem is that the clothes have no emperor.

Anna Quindlen

I must say that Kennedy's victory in Wisconsin was a triumph for democracy. It proves that a millionaire has just as good a chance as anybody else.

Bob Hope

Dan Quayle taught the kids a valuable lesson: if you don't study you could wind up Vice President.

Jay Leno

The Soviet Union will remain a one-party nation even if an opposition party were permitted – because everyone would join that party.

Ronald Reagan

If there had been any formidable body of cannibals in the country, Harry Truman would have promised to provide them with free missionaries fattened at the taxpayer's expense.

H. L. Mencken

Michael Heseltine chairs a cabinet committee looking like the last hairdresser to leave Streatham Locarno before the headlights are turned off.

Phillip Oppenheim

Hoover, if elected, will do one thing that is almost incomprehensible to the human mind: he will make a great man out of Coolidge.

Herbert Hoover

True terror is to wake up one morning and discover that your high school class is running the country.

Kurt Vonnegut

I don't have a bad word to say about anybody. Even Adolf Hitler – he was the best in his field.

Buddy Hackett

Politicians are like nappies. They should be changed regularly and for the same reason.

Patrick Murray

The only good thing I know of Cranmer is that he burned well.

Richard Froude

John Major is marginally better than cystitis.

Jo Brand

Quoting Ronald Reagan accurately is called mud-slinging.

Walter Mondale

I have faults but being wrong isn't one of them.

Jimmy Hoffa

Cass's expense account showed that he not only did the labour of several men at the same time; but that he often did it at several places, many hundreds of miles apart at the same time.

Abraham Lincoln

There are two politicians drowning and you are allowed to save only one. What do you do? Read a newspaper or eat your lunch?

Mort Sahl

Any American who is prepared to run for president should automatically, by definition be disqualified from ever doing so.

Gore Vidal

The House of Lords is a model of how to care for the elderly.

Frank Field

The news of President Eisenhower's campaigning for Richard Nixon depresses me. After a clear record of eight years, I hate to see him involved in politics.

Mort Sahl

The Democratic Party is like a mule – without pride of ancestry or hope of posterity.

Edmund Burke

Now that I am no longer President, I find that I do not win every golf game I play.

George Bush

Although He is regularly asked to do so, God does not take sides in American politics.

George Mitchell

It isn't pollution that is harming the environment. It's the impurities in our air and water that are doing it.

Dan Quayle

I am not part of the problem. I am a Republican.

Dan Quayle

A lower voter turnout is an indication that fewer people are going to the polls.

Dan Quayle

I have made good judgements in the past; I have made good judgements in the future.

Dan Quayle

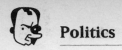

Republicans understand the importance of bondage between a mother and a child.

Dan Quayle

You can't fight City Hall but you can crap on the steps and run like mad.

Alexei Sayle

Vote early and vote often.

Al Capone

Never forget your photographer when visiting a hospital – there may always be a patient who can manage a smile.

Virginia Bottomley

We are ready for any unforeseen event that may or may not occur.

Dan Quayle

Gladstone has not got one redeeming defect.

Benjamin Disraeli

Disraeli is a self-made man who worships his creator.

John Bright

Lloyd George never saw a belt without hitting under it.

Margot Asquith

Neville Chamberlain saw foreign policy through the wrong end of a municipal drainpipe.

David Lloyd-George

If Lenin's widow does not behave, we will appoint someone
else as Lenin's widow.

Josef Stalin

There are so many sons-of-bitches in the United States that
they are entitled to some representation in Congress.

Calvin Coolidge

The Marxist law of distribution of wealth is that shortages
will be divided equally among the peasants.

John Guftason

Power corrupts. Absolute power is kind of neat.

John Lehman

Things are more like they are now than they have ever been
before.

Dwight D. Eisenhower

President Bush didn't say that. He was reading what was
given to him in a speech.

Richard Darman

History will be kind to me for I intend to write it.

Winston Churchill

One word sums up the responsibility of any vice-president,
and that word is "to be prepared".

Dan Quayle

Politics has become so expensive that it takes a lot of money even to be defeated.

Will Rogers

To say nothing especially when speaking is half the art of diplomacy.

Will Durant

It had all the hallmarks of a CIA operation; the bomb killed everybody in the room except the intended target.

William F. Buckley

Politics is derived from two words – poly, meaning many, and tics, meaning small blood-sucking insects.

Chris Clayton

Ted Kennedy. Good senator, but a bad date. You know what I'm saying folks?

Denis Leary

The trouble with fighting for human freedom is that you have to spend much of your life defending sons-of-bitches.

H. L. Mencken

Politics would be a helluva good business if it weren't for the people.

Richard Nixon

There are only a few original jokes and most of them are in Congress.

Will Rogers

We want a few mad people – look where the sane ones have landed us.

George Bernard Shaw

There is no distinctly native American criminal class except Congress.

Mark Twain

What a mess we are in now – peace has broken out.

Napoleon Bonaparte

When they asked George Washington for his ID, he just took out a quarter.

Steven Wright

Long ago I proposed that unsuccessful candidates for the Presidency be quietly hanged as a matter of public sanitation.

H. L. Mencken

I'm not going to let a group of power-mongering political men with short penises tell me what to do.

Doris Allen

I wouldn't piss down Jerry Brown's throat if his heart was on fire.

James Carville

I believe we are on an irreversible trend towards more freedom and democracy. But that could change.

Dan Quayle

Yesterday upon the stair, I met a man who wasn't there. He wasn't there again today; I think he's from the CIA.

Wright Stevens

It is indeed fitting that we gather here today to pay tribute to Abraham Lincoln, who was born in a log cabin that he built with his own hands.

Ronald Reagan

One day the don't-knows will get in and then where will we be?

Spike Milligan

It is no exaggeration to say that the undecideds could go one way or the other.

George Bush

Bill Clinton is going to try to expand his lead on female voters, one at a time.

Alex Castellanos

Politicians who lose elections should be executed. People would then think twice about running for office.

Mike Royko

The vice president simply presides over the Senate and sits around hoping for a funeral.

Harry Truman

I don't like people who use good looking young women in such a way that they end up at the bottom of rivers or lakes. Nor do I particularly care for people who cheat on their exams at Harvard. Nor do I particularly like obesity, but other than that I have no special feelings one way or the other about Teddy Kennedy.

John Simon

A politician will double cross that bridge when he comes to it.

Oscar Levant

Polls are for dogs.

John Diefenbaker

We are now approaching Washington airport. Please fasten your seat belts, adjust your watches and would Senator Kennedy return the hostess to the upright position.

Mort Sahl

I see President and Mrs. Clinton are not here tonight. Probably somewhere testifying.

Don Imus

Never vote for the best candidate – vote for the one who will do the least harm.

Frank Dane

Mr. Speaker, I withdraw my statement that half the cabinet are asses. Half the cabinet are not asses.

Benjamin Disraeli

Politics is show business for ugly people.

Paul Begala

Winston Churchill has written four volumes about himself and called it World Crisis.

A. J. Balfour

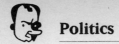

Politics

Congressmen are so damned dumb, they could throw
themselves on the ground and miss.

James Traficant

Religion

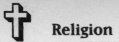

Religion

The English church-goer prefers a severe preacher because he thinks a few home truths will do his neighbours no harm.
George Bernard Shaw

Forgive my not passing any opinions on heaven and hell. You see I have friends in both places.
Jean Cocteau

God knew from all eternity that I was going to be Pope. You think he would have made me more photogenic.
Pope John XXIII

In making a sermon, think up a good beginning, then think up a good ending and finally bring these two as close together as you possibly can.
Frederick Temple

If man is only a little lower than the angels, then the angels should reform.
Mary W. Little

Extremist Catholics and extremist Protestants in Northern Ireland are getting together to get rid of ecumenism.
Patrick Murray

An archbishop is a Christian ecclesiastic of a rank superior to that attained by Christ.
H. L. Mencken

God has Alzheimer's and has forgotten about us.
Jane Wagner

Religion

A Christian is a man who feels repentance on a Sunday for
what he did on Saturday and is going to do on Monday.

Thomas Ybarra

You have no idea how much nastier I would be if I were not
a Catholic. Without supernatural aid I would hardly be a
human being.

Evelyn Waugh

Diane Keaton believes in God. But she also believes that the
radio works because there are tiny people inside it.

Woody Allen

God seems to have left the phone off the hook.

Arthur Koestler

There is no good reason why good cannot triumph as often
as evil. The triumph of anything is a matter of organisation. If
there are such things as angels, I hope they are organised
along the lines of the Mafia.

Kurt Vonnegut

The better sort of cannibals have been Christian for many
years and will not eat human flesh uncooked during Lent,
without special and costly dispensation from their bishop.

Evelyn Waugh

English Catholics are just Protestants, protesting against
Protestantism.

D. H. Lawrence

✝ Religion

A Christian is one who believes that the New Testament is a divinely inspired book, admirably suited to the spiritual needs of his neighbours.

Ambrose Bierce

It is no accident that the symbol of a bishop is a crook and the symbol of an archbishop is a double-cross.

Gregory Dix

Never be alone in a lift with a man who has religious tracts on his desk.

Pam Brown

She believed in nothing; only her scepticism kept her from being an atheist.

Jean-Paul Sartre

An atheist is a man who has no invisible means of support.

Fulton J. Sheen

God is everywhere, even though we can't see Him. He's the one who opens the doors at the supermarket.

George Anderson

While people may not be a great deal wiser after my sermons, they are always a great deal older.

W. R. Inge

You are not an agnostic, Paddy. You are just a fat slob who is too lazy to go to Mass.

Conor Cruise O'Brien

Religion ✝

It is recommended for your soul's sake to do each day two things you dislike. It is a precept that I have followed scrupulously. For every day I have got up and I have gone to bed.

Somerset Maugham

Women give themselves to God when the devil wants nothing more to do with them.

Sophie Arnould

Let it appear in trial that the accused is a Sunday school superintendent and the jury says guilty almost automatically.

H. L. Mencken

The Protestant churches look after you from birth to death – the Catholic church looks after you from conception to resurrection.

Joe Foyle

The Jews have produced only three original geniuses: Christ, Spinoza and myself.

Gertrude Stein

Presbyterianism is not a religion for gentlemen.

King Charles II

A lady's husband seeks compensation by reading the lessons in church with great gusto, particularly such passages as deal with fornication.

Douglas Sutherland

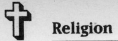

If I could just see a miracle. Just one miracle. If I could see a burning bush or the seas part or my Uncle Sacha pick up a cheque.

Woody Allen

I used to be in favour of women priests, but two years in the Cabinet cured me of them.

Norman St. John-Stevas

If Dorothy Thompson doesn't know as much as God, she most certainly knows as much as He did at her age.

Ilka Chase

Elizabeth the First was as just and merciful as Nero and as good a Christian as Mahomet.

John Wesley

Call me old-fashioned, but I am a deeply religious woman. That is to say, I firmly believe there is something Up There and I'm sure most women feel the same from time to time.

Edna Everage

Dean Inge thought that the Kingdom of Heaven was confined to people who had taken a first class degree at Oxford or Cambridge.

Sidney Dark

Yes I admit Jesus was Jewish – but only on his mother's side.

Archie Bunker

The Church of England is the perfect church for those who don't go to church.

Gerald Priestland

Poor soul, very sad; her late husband, you know, a very sad death – eaten by missionaries – poor soul.

William A. Spooner

My car is God's way of telling me to slow down.

Dick Sharples

My parents sent me to an interfaith camp where I was beaten up by boys of all races and religions.

Woody Allen

If you cross an agnostic with a Jehovah Witness, you get a fellow who knocks on your door for no particular reason.

Blanche Knott

I would prefer Heaven for climate but Hell for society as all my friends are Protestant.

Father Healy

God made Adam before Eve because he didn't want any advice on the matter.

Patrick Murray

The good people sleep much better than the bad people. Of course the bad people enjoy the waking hours much more.

Woody Allen

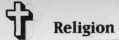

Conscience is the inner voice which warns us that somebody may be looking.

H. L. Mencken

Repent or be damned. If you have already repented, please disregard this notice.

Patrick Murray

Making fun of born-again Christians is like hunting dairy cows with a high-powered rifle and scope.

P. J. O'Rourke

I always carry a bullet in my breast pocket because it saved my life. In a fight somebody hurled a bible at me and to my good fortune it ricocheted off the bullet.

Woody Allen

There are several good precautions against temptation but the surest is cowardice.

Mark Twain

I have nothing against the Jesuits but I wouldn't like my daughter to marry one.

Patrick Murray

I don't know if God exists, but it would be better for His reputation if He didn't.

Jules Renard

During the last ten years, I have stolen seventy-five bibles, perhaps the national record.

H. L. Mencken

The vices of the clergy are far less dangerous than their virtues.
Edward Gibbon

A Christian is one who follows the teachings of Christ insofar as they are not inconsistent with a life of sin.
Ambrose Bierce

I am a born again atheist.
Gore Vidal

There's one born again every minute.
P. J. O'Rourke

If in the last few years you haven't discarded a major opinion or acquired a new one, check your pulse. You may be dead.
Gelet Burgess

There are 869 different forms of lying but only one of them has been squarely forbidden: Thou shalt not bear false witness against thy neighbour.
Mark Twain

In matters of marriage or religion I never give advice, for I will have no man's torment in this world or the next laid to my charge.
Lord Chesterfield

All this fuss about women priests. Most of them look like men anyway and the male priests have been wearing dresses for years. If they had kept quiet about it, nobody would have noticed the difference.
Warren Mitchell

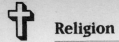

Some people go to church only when they are being
baptized, married or buried – hatched, matched and
dispatched.

James Hewett

I am never molested when travelling alone on trains. There
are just a few words I have to say and I am immediately left
alone. They are "Are you a born-again Christian?"

Rita Rudner

I've been reading in an Alabama newspaper that one man
shot another man dead because he beat him in a Bible-
quoting competition.

Richard Dawkins

I was driving along one day and I saw a hitchhiker with a
sign saying Heaven. So I hit him.

Steven Wright

One of the proofs of the divinity of our gospel is that it has
survived preaching.

Woodrow Wilson

An Archbishop is a Christian ecclesiastic of a rank superior
to that attained by Christ.

H. L. Mencken

Samuel Beckett would have made a marvellous pope. True
he was a Protestant and did not believe in God, but these are
incidentals.

John Carey

For Catholics, death is a promotion.

Cliff Gorman

Life after death is as improbable as sex after marriage.

Madeline Kahn

Perhaps the most revolting character that the United States ever produced was the Christian business man.

H. L. Mencken

Immortality is the condition of a dead man who does not believe he is dead.

H. L. Mencken

Science and Technology

Science and Technology

Only two things are infinite – the universe and human stupidity and I'm not sure about the former.

Albert Einstein

The more modern and stream-lined aircraft become, the more they resemble those paper arrows we made at school.

Ashley Cooper

The atomic bomb will not go off – and I speak as an expert in explosives.

William Leahy

Scientists have come up with a fantastic invention for looking through solid walls. It's called a window.

Richard Feynman

Psychologists are scientists about as much as converted savages are Christians.

Georges Politzer

Scientists have odious manners, except when you prop up their theory; then you can borrow money from them.

Mark Twain

Any man who grows to be more than five feet seven inches is a weed.

Frank Lloyd Wright

I'm going to keep taking pot-shots at the birds on my lawn until the bastards learn to shit green.

W. C. Fields

Science and Technology

The world was created on 22nd October, 4004 BC at six
o'clock in the evening.

James Ussher

The survival of several wild bird species is dependent on
burned toast.

Faith Hines

I took a lie detector test the other day. No I didn't.

Steven Wright

If you share a flat with a biologist, don't eat anything in the
fridge.

Faith Hines

My father invented the burglar alarm – which unfortunately
was stolen from him.

Victor Borge

Noah was an amateur; the Titanic was built by professionals.

Malcolm Allison

Cold? If the thermometer had been an inch longer we
would all have frozen to death.

Mark Twain

If it squirms, it's biology; if it stinks it's chemistry; if it doesn't
work it's physics and if you can't understand it, it's
mathematics.

Magnus Pyke

As a graduate of the Zsa Zsa Gabor School of Creative
Mathematics, I honestly do not know how old I am.

Erma Bombeck

Researchers have already cast much darkness on this subject
and if they continue their investigations we shall soon know
nothing at all about it.

Mark Twain

I worry about scientists discovering that lettuce has been
fattening all along.

Erma Bombeck

If trees could scream, would we be so cavalier about cutting
them down? We might if they screamed all the time and for
no good reason.

Jack Handey

Hofstadter's Law states that it always takes longer than you
expect, even when you take into account Hofstadter's Law.

Douglas Hofstadter

A friend of mine once sent me a postcard with a picture of
the entire planet Earth taken from space. On the back it said
"Wish you were here".

Steven Wright

Last week I bought a new phone. I took it out of the box,
hooked it up to the wall and pressed redial. The phone had a
nervous breakdown.

Steven Wright

I had all my electric cords shortened to save on electricity.
Gracie Allen

High insurance rates are really what killed the dinosaurs.
David Letterman

I often put boiling water in the freezer. Then whenever I need boiling water, I simply defrost it.
Gracie Allen

Don't let me catch anyone talking about the Universe in my department.
Ernest Rutherford

Every so often I like to stick my head out the window, look up and smile for a satellite picture.
Steven Wright

In my house there's this light switch that doesn't do anything. Every so often I would flick it on and off just to check. Yesterday I got a call from a woman in Germany. She said "Cut it out".
Steven Wright

There is a theory which states that if ever anybody discovers exactly what the Universe is for and why it is here, it will instantly disappear and be replaced by something even more bizarre and inexplicable. There is another theory which states that this has already happened.
Douglas Adams

My theory of evolution is that Darwin was adopted.

> *Steven Wright*

They x-rayed my head and found nothing.

> *Jerome Dean*

I had some eyeglasses. I was walking down the street when suddenly the prescription ran out.

> *Steven Wright*

I think there is a world market for maybe five computers.

> *Thomas Watson (1943)*

The telegraph is a kind of very long cat. You pull his tail in New York and his head is mewing in Los Angeles. Radio operates in exactly the same way, except that there is no cat.

> *Albert Einstein*

The Internet is like a herd of performing elephants with diarrhoea – massive, difficult to redirect, awe-inspiring, entertaining and a source of mindboggling amounts of excrement when you least expect it.

> *Gene Spafford*

If I have not seen as far as others, it is because giants were standing on my shoulders.

> *Hal Abelson*

Science and Technology

The most important thing about a programming language is the name. A language will not succeed without a name. I have recently invented a very good name and I am looking for a suitable language.

Donald Knuth

Close the hatch. Careful not to lock it on the way.

Buzz Aldrin

Hardware is the part of the computer that can be kicked.

Jeff Pesis

The two most abundant things in the universe are hydrogen and stupidity.

Harlan Ellison

I used to be an airline pilot. I got fired because I kept locking the keys in the plane. They caught me on an eighty-foot step ladder with a coat hanger.

Steven Wright

I used to think that the human brain was the most fascinating part of the body and then I realised, "what is telling me that?"

Emo Philips

When the guy who made the first drawing board got it wrong, what did he go back to?

Steven Wright

Science and Technology

All modern men are descended from wormlike creatures, but it shows more on some people.

Will Cuppy

It takes more hot water to make cold water hot than it takes to make hot water cold.

Larry Dowd

The best way to accelerate a Macintosh is at 9.8 m/sec^2.

Marcus Dolengo

When graphing a function, the width of the line should be inversely proportional to the precision of the data.

Marvin J. Albinak

A human being is just a computer's way of building another computer: usually a better one. That is why computers will never replace human beings. We are their sex organs.

David Gerrold

Imagine if every Thursday your shoes exploded if you tied them in the usual way. This happens all the time with computers and nobody thinks of complaining.

Jeff Raskin

The Internet is so big, so powerful and so pointless that for some people it is a complete substitute for life.

Andrew Brown

A couple of months in the laboratory can frequently save a couple of hours in the library.

Frank Westheimer

One of the main causes of the fall of the Roman Empire was that, lacking zero, they had no way to indicate successful termination of their C programs.

Robert Firth

My computer may be slow but it's hard to use.

Don Geddis

The moon may be smaller than the earth, but it's further away.

Steven Wright

To say that a gram of plutonium could kill everyone on the planet is like saying that one drop of sperm could impregnate all of the women in China.

Tom Orth

If you can keep your head while those about you are losing theirs, have you considered becoming a guillotine operator?

Don Geddis

Becoming extinct is a perfect answer to everything and I defy anybody to think of a better.

Will Cuppy

Botany is the art of insulting flowers in Latin and Greek.

Alphonse Karr

Think of the poor old lady who had her petrol tank removed from her car and had it replaced with one that held litres instead of gallons.

Kenneth Manning

A computer is like an Old Testament god, with a lot of rules and no mercy.

Joseph Campbell

I think we all felt the same way when the shuttle blew up. Damn, I forgot to set my VCR. Now I'm going to have to borrow the tape.

Denis Leary

Beware of bugs in the above code – I have only proved it correct, not tried it.

Donald Knuth

If I had thought about it, I wouldn't have done the experiment. The literature was full of examples that said you can't do this.

Spencer Silver

I've just heard that photons have mass. I didn't even know they were Catholics.

Don Geddis

If man evolved from the ape, how come there are still apes about? Some of them were given choices.

Johnny Hart

You know your science teacher is nuts if he says the "c" in $E=mc^2$ stands for carrot.

David Letterman

Pigeons are just rats with wings.

Alfred Small

Who is the designer genius who puts frosted glass in the toilet windows of airplanes?

Harry Scott

We have already hunted the grey whale into extinction twice.

Andrea Arnold

I figure you have the same chance of winning the lottery whether you play or not.

Fran Lebowitz

Ants are wonderful creatures – they have their own police force and army, but no navy.

Mrs. Patrick Campbell

The secret of creativity is knowing how to hide your sources.

Albert Einstein

I cannot smell mothballs because it's so difficult to get their little legs apart.

Steve Martin

Social Behaviour and Manners

Social Behaviour and Manners

A gentleman never insults someone unintentionally.

Oscar Wilde

Love your enemies – it will drive them nuts.

Eleanor Doan

One can survive anything nowadays except death and live down anything except a good reputation.

Oscar Wilde

One nice thing about egotists – they don't talk much about other people.

Lucille S. Harper

It ain't no sin if you crack a few laws now and then, just so long as you don't break any.

Mae West

Early to rise and early to bed, makes a man healthy, wealthy and dead.

James Thurber

Why be disagreeable, when with a little effort you can be impossible?

Douglas Woodruff

You will always find a few Eskimos ready to tell the Congolese how to cope with the heat.

Stanislaw Lec

Social Behaviour and Manners

When you are in trouble, people calling to sympathise are really only looking for the particulars.

Edgar Howe

Be nice to people on your way up, because you'll meet 'em on your way down.

Wilson Mizner

Some things never change – like my underwear.

Rod Stewart

Please don't ask me to relax. It's only the tension that's holding me together.

Helen Murray

If you wait for a repairman, you will wait all day. If you go out for five minutes, he will arrive and leave while you are gone.

Arthur Bloch

Modesty is the hope that other people will discover by themselves how wonderful we really are.

Aldo Cammarota

The person who agrees with everything you say either isn't listening to you or plans to sell you something.

Bud Holiday

Give me the luxuries of life and I will willingly do without the necessities.

Frank Lloyd Wright

My idea of an agreeable person is a person who agrees with me.

Benjamin Disraeli

We shall never be content until each man makes his own weather and keeps it to himself.

Jerome K. Jerome

Suburbia is where the developer bulldozes out the trees and then names the streets after them.

Bill Vaughan

People who mean well – always a poisonous class.

E. V. Lucas

Whenever you meet a public man who ostentatiously shortens his forename, make the sign of the Evil Eye and count your spoons.

Bernard Levin

Beware of the naked man who offers you his shirt.

Harvey MacKay

There will be a rain dance on Friday, weather permitting.

George Carlin

God in his bounty and generosity always creates more horses' asses than there are horses to attach to them.

Thomas Perry

If you don't drink, smoke or drive a car, you're a tax evader.

Tom Foley

If a man sits down to think, he is immediately asked if he has a headache.

Ralph W. Emerson

How is it that the person in front of you at the supermarket checkout always has one item that requires a summit conference?

Jo Ann Thomas

An inferiority complex would be a blessing if only the right people had it.

Alan Reed

Your right to wear a mint-green polyester leisure suit ends where it meets my eyes.

Fran Lebowitz

The best way to convince a fool that he is wrong is to let him have his own way.

Josh Billings

If one is shot dead, it is a great consolation to know that it was with a legally held fire-arm.

Margaret Thatcher

It was that sort of house where they have six Bibles and no corkscrew.

Mark Twain

A lot of people never use their initiative because nobody ever tells them to.

Mary Allen

The trouble with giving advice is that people want to repay you.

James Dent

If you must commit suicide, always contrive to do it as decorously as possible; the decencies, whether of life or of death, should never be lost sight of.

George Borrow

It is an important general rule always to refer to your friend's country establishment as a cottage.

Stephen Potter

There are no exceptions to the rule that everybody likes to be an exception to the rule.

Malcolm Forbes

There is only one thing worse than being talked about and that is not being talked about.

Oscar Wilde

I believe only in the SEBF Association. Screw Everybody But Fields.

W. C. Fields

When my bridge partner excused himself to go to the bathroom, it was the only time all night I knew what he had in his hand.

George Kaufman

Applause is the custom of showing one's pleasure at beautiful music by immediately following it with an ugly noise.

Percy A. Scholes

The sight of a gibbet in the wilds of Central Africa gave me infinite pleasure as it proved I was in a civilised society.

Mungo Park

Never lend books, for no one ever returns them; the only books I have in my library are the books that other folks have lent me.

Anatole France

Anyone who lies about Gore Vidal is doing him a kindness.

William F. Buckley

Male criminal offenders, at least those who are caught, have an IQ below the average.

Lewis Wolpert

If you cannot get people to listen to you any other way, tell them it's confidential.

Patrick Murray

I'm never going to be famous. My name will never be writ large on the roster of those who do things. I don't do anything. Not one single thing. I used to bite my nails. I don't even do that any more.

Dorothy Parker

There is a serious tendency towards capitalism among the well-to-do peasants.

Mao Tse-Tung

The denunciation of the young is a necessary part of the hygiene of older people and greatly assists the circulation of the blood.

Logan P. Smith

The only hour in the normal day that is more pleasurable than the hour spent in bed with a book before going to sleep is the hour spent in bed with a book after being called in the morning.

Rose Macaulay

When I roomed with Simon Hobday in South Africa, he designated Monday as washday. That meant filling a bath with water, pouring in a liberal amount of detergent, emptying in the entire contents of his suitcase and then proceeding to stir the lot with a putter. When he felt the clothes had been stirred sufficiently, they were thrown out on to the balcony to dry.

Roddy Carr

I belong to that section of the class which makes the upper half of the class possible.

Julius Cohen

Humpty Dumpty sat on a wall, Humpty Dumpty has a great
fall. Three male Hispanics were seen leaving the area.

Colin Quinn

No visit to Dove Cottage, Grasmere, is complete without
examining the outhouse where Hazlitt's father, a Unitarian
minister of strong liberal views, attempted to put his hand up
Dorothy Wordsworth's skirt.

Alan Coren

New York is the Land of Genetic Close Calls. There are a lot
of people who missed being another species by one
chromosome. Look, that guy could have been a badger.

Kevin Rooney

With a heavy step Sir Matthew left the room and spent the
morning designing mausoleums for his enemies.

Eric Linklater

When you are alone with Max Beerbohm, he takes off his
face and reveals his mask.

Oscar Wilde

Go to bed. Whatever you are staying up late for isn't worth
it.

Andy Rooney

Aristocrats spend their childhood being beaten by fierce
nannies and their later years murdering wildlife, so it is hardly
surprising their sex-lives are a bit cock-eyed.

Jilly Cooper

Always acknowledge a fault frankly. This will throw those in authority off their guard and give you opportunity to commit more.

Mark Twain

Everybody hates me because I'm so universally liked.

Peter De Vries

Experience teaches you that the man who looks you straight in the eye, particularly if he adds a firm handshake, is hiding something.

Clifton Fadiman

Just the other day in the Underground I enjoyed the pleasure of offering my seat to three ladies.

G. K. Chesterton

I don't answer the telephone because I have this feeling there is going to be somebody on the other end.

Fred Couples

I do not need the assistance of a translator to offer a toast to this gracious lady, Mrs Dean Rusk. Up your bottom, madam.

Andrei Gromyko

He knew the precise psychological moment when to say nothing.

Oscar Wilde

I am controversial, but only among people who don't share my views.

J. K. Galbraith

Blessed is he who, having nothing to say abstains from giving evidence of that fact.

George Eliot

Success didn't spoil me; I've always been insufferable.

Fran Lebowitz

I did not suspect it was an orgy until three days later.

S. J. Perelman

There is no pleasure in having nothing to do; the fun is in having lots to do and not doing it.

Mary Little

He is as good as his word – and his word is no good.

Seamas MacManus

I once got a Christmas job in a department store as Santa Claus. A little girl rushed up to me and said, "Hello, Father Christmas." I replied "Bugger off, I'm not on duty until eleven."

W. C. Fields

There is no human problem which could not be solved if people would simply do as I advise.

Gore Vidal

Social Behaviour and Manners

I have never understood why anybody agreed to go on being a rustic after about 1400.

Kingsley Amis

Whenever a friend succeeds, a little something in me dies.

Gore Vidal

People are not born bastards. They have to work at it.

Rod McKuen

The only reason they say "women and children first" is to test the strength of the lifeboats.

Judy Allen

Never learn to do anything: if you don't learn, you always find someone else to do it for you.

Mark Twain

I once gave a waiter a tip – I told him never to step off a moving bus.

Groucho Marx

I talk to myself a lot. That bothers some people because I use a megaphone.

Steven Wright

I know that's a secret, for it's whispered everywhere.

William Congreve

A person seldom falls sick, but the bystanders are animated with a faint hope that he will die.

Ralph Waldo Emerson

Heiresses are never jilted.

George Meredith

I was humble for a fortnight, but nobody noticed

Katharine Whitehorn

I could see that, if not actually disgruntled, he was far from gruntled.

P. G. Wodehouse

Most people who cheat on fares in the Underground do so because of an unresolved castration complex.

Darian Leader

I believe in loyalty. When a woman reaches an age she likes, she should stick to it.

Eva Gabor

Princess Diana wears more clothes in one day than Gandhi wore in his entire life.

Joan Rivers

Develop your eccentricities while you are young. That way, when you are old, people won't think you're going ga-ga.

David Ogilvy

Listen to me, Your Lordship. You have broken my business, you have ruined my home, you have sent my son to prison and my wife to a dishonoured grave and you have seduced my only daughter. But have a care, Lord FitzWallop, I am a man of quick temper. Do not try me too far.

Horace Wyndam

There are only two actions I cannot tolerate. One is the act of beginning a sentence and refusing to finish it. The other is murder.

Lucille Kallen

The human race is a race of cowards: and I am not only marching in that procession but carrying a banner.

Mark Twain

Let me have my own way in exactly everything, and a sunnier and more pleasant creature does not exist.

Thomas Carlyle

I found out that it's not good to talk about my troubles. Eighty per cent of the people who hear them don't care and the other twenty per cent are glad you're having trouble.

Tommy Lasorda

I am not at the front, Madam, fighting for civilisation, because I am the civilisation for which they are fighting.

Lytton Strachey

Most people who are as attractive, witty and intellligent as I am are usually conceited.

Joan Rivers

To me it's a good idea to always carry two sacks of something when you walk around. That way, if anybody says, "Hey, can you give me a hand?", you can say, "Sorry, got these sacks".

Jack Handey

I am the only person to have been blown off a lavatory during the blitz while reading Jane Austen.

Kingsley Martin

It takes your enemy and your friend, working together, to hurt you to the heart; the one to slander you and the other to tell you the news.

Mark Twain

I have been friendly with Brendan Behan only in the hope that I would be free from the horror of his acquaintanceship.

Patrick Kavanagh

Herbert Beerbohm Tree is a charming fellow, and so clever: he models himself on me.

Oscar Wilde

Did you ever get a letter from Monty James? I once had a note from him inviting us to dinner – we guessed that the time was eight and not three, as it appeared to be, but all we could tell about the day was that it was not Wednesday.

George Lyttleton

Allow me to put the record straight. I'm forty-six and have been for some years past.

Erica Jong

I have often wished I had time to cultivate modesty, but I am too busy thinking about myself.

Edith Sitwell

Actually, there is no way of making vomiting courteous. You have to do the next best thing, which is to vomit in such a way that the story you tell about it later will be amusing.

P. J. O'Rourke

If other people are going to talk, conversation becomes impossible.

James McNeill Whistler

Wearing underwear is as formal as I ever hope to get.

Ernest Hemingway

Lady Peabury was in the morning room reading a novel; early training gave a guilty spice to this recreation, for she had been brought up to believe that to read a novel before luncheon was one of the gravest sins it was possible for a gentlewoman to commit.

Evelyn Waugh

I have a new book coming out. It's a self help book called *How to Get Along with Everyone*. I wrote it with this other asshole.

Steve Martin

I think you should defend to the death the right of the Ku Klux Klan to march and then go down to meet them with baseball bats.

Woody Allen

Sheets can be kept clean by getting drunk and falling asleep with your clothes on.

P. J. O'Rourke

Few things are harder to put up with than the annoyance of a good example.

Mark Twain

Most of the stuff told to you in confidence you couldn't get anyone else to listen to.

F. P. Adams

I live on a very rough council estate. The rag and bone man stopped yesterday for a pint of lager outside our local. When he came out his horse was on bricks.

Roy Brown

There's a new charity I'm involved with called Help a London Child – Kill a Social Worker.

Alexei Sayle

Passionate hatred can give meaning and purpose to an empty life.

Eric Hoffer

My uncle had a rabbit's foot for thirty years. His other foot was quite normal.

Tom Griffin

Social Behaviour and Manners

The more things a man is ashamed of, the more respectable he is.

George Bernard Shaw

You'll never catch a nudist with his pants down.

David Letterman

We are here on earth to do good for others. What the others are here for I don't know.

W. H. Auden

A friend is someone who will help you move; a good friend is someone who will help you move a body.

Alexei Sayle

I always astonish strangers by my amiability, because no human being could be so disagreeable as they expect me to be.

George Bernard Shaw

I'm all into self improvement – I turn my underwear inside out once a week.

Richard Crowley

You simply must stop taking advice from other people.

Melissa Timberman

Man invented language to satisfy his deep need to complain.

Lily Tomlin

If you go long enough without a bath, even the fleas will let you alone.

Ernie Pyle

There are few situations in life that cannot be resolved promptly, and to the satisfaction of all concerned, by either suicide, a bag of gold or thrusting the despised antagonist over a precipice on a dark night.

Ernest Bramah

May God defend me from my friends. I can defend myself from my enemies.

Voltaire

A man who for an entire week does nothing but hit himself over the head has little reason to be proud.

Stanislaw Lem

To consult is to seek another's advice on a course already decided upon.

Ambrose Bierce

People who insist on telling their dreams are among the terrors of the breakfast table.

Max Beerbohm

Never trust a man who speaks well of everyone.

John Collins

Beware of all enterprises that require new clothes.

Henry Thoreau

If I knew that a man was coming to my house with the conscious design of doing me good, I should run for my life.

Henry Thoreau

Don't bother telling people your troubles. Half of them don't care and the other half figure you probably had it coming.

Josh Billings

A gossip is one who talks to you about other people. A bore is one who talks to you about himself. A brilliant conversationalist is one who talks to you about yourself.

William King

I don't know whether the world is full of smart men bluffing or imbeciles who mean it.

Morrie Brickman

A true friend always stabs you in the front.

Oscar Wilde

Of all the unbearable nuisances, the ignoramus that has travelled is the worst.

Kin Hubbard

People are far more sincere and good humoured at speeding their parting guests than on meeting them.

Anton Chekhov

I cannot figure out streakers. I guess it's just their way of showing they're nuts.

Larry Glick

I was full of fire in my youth. I had to carry fire insurance until I was over forty.

W. C. Fields

I asked her what she was doing on Saturday night and when she said "committing suicide", I asked her what she was doing on Friday night.

Woody Allen

I did not attend his funeral, but I wrote a nice letter saying I approved of it.

Mark Twain

I'm going to memorise your name and throw my head away.

Oscar Levant

If I die I'm sorry for all the bad things I did to you. And if I live I'm sorry for all the bad things I'm going to do to you.

Roy Scheider

If I were not afraid my people would keep it out of the newspapers, I should commit suicide tomorrow.

Max Beerbohm

When there are two conflicting versions of a story, the wisest course is to believe the one in which people appear at their worst.

H. Allen Smith

Revenge is a dish which people of taste prefer to eat cold.

Dennis Price

Think twice before you speak to a friend in need.

Ambrose Bierce

When I die they will write in the newspapers that the sons-of-bitches of this world have lost their leader.

Vincent Gardenia

Self respect is the secure feeling that no one, as yet, is suspicious.

H. L. Mencken

The man who would call a spade a spade should be compelled to use one: it is the only thing he is fit for.

Oscar Wilde

Sport

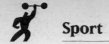

A coarse golfer is one who has to shout "fore" before he putts.

Michael Green

I promised I'd take Rotherham out of the second division. I did – into the third division.

Tommy Docherty

The English cricket team have just three problems. They cannot bat, they cannot bowl and they cannot field.

Rodney Marsh

I do not participate in any sport that has ambulances at the bottom of the hill.

Erma Bombeck

The chances of a rematch for Lewis are slim and none. And slim is out of town.

Don King

Pete Sampras does have a weakness. He cannot cook for a start.

Michael Chang

I hate all sports as rabidly as a person who likes sports hates common sense.

H. L. Mencken

I don't think the discus will ever attract any interest until we start throwing them at each other.

Al Oerter

Joggers are basically neurotic, bony, smug types who could bore the paint off a DC-10. It is a scientifically proven fact that having to sit through a three-minute conversation between two joggers will cause your IQ to drop thirteen points.

Rick Reilly

I wanted to have a career in sports when I was young, but I had to give it up. I'm only six feet tall, so I couldn't play basketball. I'm only 190 pounds, so I couldn't play football and I have 20-20 vision so I couldn't be a referee.

Jay Leno

The only England captain to have led a team which scored fewer than forty-six runs in a Test match was Arthur Shrewsbury and he shot himself.

Ian Wooldridge

The first time I went skiing I wasn't very good at it, so I broke a leg. Thank goodness it wasn't one of mine.

Michael Green

When primitive man beat the ground with sticks, they called it witchcraft. When modern man does the same thing, they call it golf.

Michael Neary

I've just played World War Two golf – out in 39 and back in 45.

Lee Trevino

I am scared of only three things – lightning, a side-hill putt and Bill Hogan.

Sam Snead

Nigel Mansell has about as much charisma as a damp spark plug.

Alan Hubbard

Football is a game designed to keep coal miners off the streets.

Jimmy Breslin

I scored a hundred on my first cricket tour – on the golf course.

Hugh Morris

As a football player at Princeton, I always felt like Dolly Parton's shoulder-straps. I knew I had an important job to do, but I felt totally incapable of doing it.

Jimmy Stewart

I never kick my ball in the rough or improve my lie in a sand trap. For that I have a caddy.

Bob Hope

There are three things a man must do alone – testify, die and putt.

Bennett Cerf

A golf ball will always travel furthest when hit in the wrong direction.

Henry Beard

The only sure rule in golf is – he who has the fastest cart never has to play the bad lie.

Mickey Mantle

It is necessary to invent quotes more and more these days because professional golfers are gradually losing the power of speech. Already adverbs have been eliminated entirely from their vocabulary. "I hit the ball super but putted just horrible."

Peter Dobereiner

When playing poker, anyone who looks at Herbert Ransom's face is cheating.

Franklin P. Adams

Man for man, on paper, the Australian side stand out like a dog's balls.

Greg Chappell

The only way to beat Nick Price is to get him drunk at altitude.

Nick Faldo

A traditional fixture at Wimbledon is the way the BBC TV commentary box fills up with British players eliminated in the early rounds.

Clive James

Real golfers, whatever the provocation, never strike the caddy with a driver. A sand wedge is far more effective.

Brian Barnes

There's no secret to winning the Indianapolis 500. You just press the accelerator to the floor and steer left.

Bill Vukovich

Sport

Winged Foot G. C. has the toughest eighteen finishing holes in golf.

Dave Marr

If you think it's difficult to meet new people, try picking up the wrong golf ball.

Jack Lemmon

This defeat has taught me a lesson, but I'm not quite sure what it is.

John McEnroe

One is always a little nervous watching England bat.

Peter May

The easiest shot in golf is the fourth putt.

Ring Lardner

If David Feherty hadn't been a golfer, he probably would have been a wringer-outer for a one-armed window cleaner.

Myles Dungan

I have been playing a twenty-seven-year-old opponent. I've got socks older than he is.

Lee Trevino

Being manager at Oldham was like being a nitroglycerine juggler.

Joe Royle

The one reward that golf has given me, and I shall always be thankful for it, is introducing me to some of the world's most picturesque, tireless and bald-faced liars.

Ring Lardner

The only thing I have against golf is that it takes you so far from the clubhouse.

Eric Linklater

Ben, would you like to know how to sink those putts? Just hit the ball a little closer to the hole.

Valerie Hogan

I think Brian Moore's teeth are the kind you buy in a DIY shop and hammer in yourself. He's the only player we have who looks like a French forward.

Paul Rendall

The only time Byron Nelson left the fairway all day was to pee in the bushes.

Jackie Burke

The less said about the putter the better. It is an instrument of torture, designed by Tantalus and forged in the devil's own smithy.

Tony Lema

You can make a lot of money out of golf. Just ask my ex-wives.

Lee Trevino

Exactly how intricate a sport is jogging? You were two years old. You ran after the cat. You pretty much had it mastered.

Rick Reilly

I shouldn't be so upset at losing to Benfica. After all, they have the best players, the best referees and the best linesmen.

Jimmy Hagan

The first time I see a jogger smiling, I'll consider it.

Joan Rivers

I've heard John Newcombe describe a tennis match and if I came close to imitating that, I believe I could impersonate a wild duck singing "Annie Laurie" underwater.

Robert Easton

There's an old saying on tour. Set fire to the trees and cover the greens with broken glass, put the pros out there in gasoline soaked pants and barefoot and someone will break par.

Tommy Bolt

Golf is the only game in the world in which a precise knowledge of the rules can earn you a reputation for bad sportsmanship.

Patrick Campbell

This was the worst golf I ever played. I couldn't hit a cow's backside with a banjo.

David Llewellyn

Of all the games man has devised, supposedly for his
enjoyment, golf is in a class by itself in the anguish it inflicts.

H. G. Wind

Some guys get so nervous playing golf for money, the greens
don't need fertilising for a year.

Dave Hill

When John L. Sullivan struck me, I felt as if a telephone pole
had been inserted in me, sideways.

Paddy Ryan

Golf is the loneliest of all games, not excluding postal chess.

Peter Dobereiner

The only way I am going to beat Jack Nicklaus is if he signs
the wrong score-card.

Lee Trevino

And there's the unmistakable figure of Joe Mercer, or is it
Lester Piggott?

Brough Scott

No one has had a golf swing like Eamon Darcy's since
Quasimodo gave up golf to concentrate on bell-ringing.

Bill Elliot

There weren't many bowling alleys that would let me come
back. I have an overhand delivery.

John Wayne

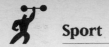

My son Rollo is exceedingly good at golf. He scores 120
every time, while Mr. Burns who is supposed to be one of
the best players in the club, seldom manages to reach 80.

P. G. Wodehouse

Given a choice between Raquel Welch and a hundred at
Lord's, I'd take the hundred every time.

Geoffrey Boycott

There's this interior linesman who's as big as a gorilla and as
strong as a gorilla. If he was as smart as a gorilla, he'd be fine.

Sam Bailey

Someone said my performance in the second half of the
Calcutta Cup match was a bit like J. P. R. Williams. In the
first half it was more like Kenneth Williams.

Jonathan Callard

Sure the fight was fixed. I fixed it with my right hand.

George Foreman

The only useful putting advice I ever got from my caddy was
to keep the ball low.

Chi Chi Rodriguez

Colin Montgomerie has the temper of a warthog recently
stung by a wasp and a face like a bull-dog licking piss off a
nettle.

David Feherty

Bryant Gumbel's ego has applied for statehood. If it's
accepted it will be the fifth largest.

Willard Scott

With my winnings this year, I intend to buy the Alamo and give it back to Mexico.

Lee Trevino

Vince Lombardi is completely fair. He treats us all the same – like dogs.

Henry Jordan

Football hooligans? Well, there are the 92 club chairmen for a start.

Brian Clough

I have consistently interpreted Law 26 of Rugby Union on "misconduct" by awarding a scrum for obscenity and a penalty for blasphemy.

Alec Charters

The roughest thing I ever said to an umpire was, "Are you sure?"

Rod Laver

I play golf in the low eighties. If it's any hotter than that, I won't play.

Joe E. Lewis

Magellan went around the world in 1521 – which isn't too many strokes when you consider the distance.

Joe Laurie

In my day there were plenty of footballers around who would knock your bollocks off. The difference was that at the end of the match they would shake your hand and help you look for them.

Nat Lofthouse

Ballesteros is the No. 1. He hits the ball further than I go on my holidays.

Lee Trevino

I am a professional tennis player. I have a friend who is a nun and her social life is better than mine.

Wendy Turnbull

There are just two types of coaches – those who have just been fired and those that are going to be fired.

Bum Phillips

The decathlon consists of nine Mickey Mouse events and a 1500 metres.

Steve Ovett

And that's the third time this session he's missed his waistcoat pocket with the chalk.

Ted Lowe

When I said "You're a disgrace to mankind", I was talking to myself, not the umpire.

John McEnroe

You can't help feeling that goalkeeper Peter Bonetti looks rather like a member of the public who just happens to have wandered on to the pitch.

Nick Hancock

A golf ball hitting a tree shall be deemed not to have hit the tree. Hitting a tree is just bad luck and has no place in a scientific game. The player should estimate the distance the ball would have travelled if it had not hit the tree and play the ball from there.

Arnie Kunz

Eamon D'Arcy has a golf swing like an octopus fallling out of a tree.

David Feherty

Eddie Waring has done for Rugby League what Cyril Smith has done for hang gliding.

Reggie Bowden

American football consists of committee meetings separated by outbreaks of violence.

George Will

If Ron "Chopper" Harris was in a good mood, he'd put iodine on his studs.

Jimmy Greaves

The fellows in the executive boxes at Everton are the lucky ones. They can draw the curtains.

Stan Boardman

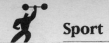

The umpire admitted to me afterwards that he had given me out LBW to Jim Parks because he was desperate for a pee.
Denis Compton

His sperm count was lower than an English cricket score.
A.A. Gill

I wouldn't ever set out to hurt anybody deliberately unless it was, you know important – like a league game or something.
Dick Butkus

I don't want to sound paranoid, but that electronic line judge knows who I am.
John McEnroe

Aye, they say the new striker I'm opposing is fast – but how fast can he limp?
Mick McCarthy

A horse is dangerous at both ends and uncomfortable in the middle.
Ian Fleming

The key to tennis is to win the last point.
Jim Courier

Give a man a fish and he eats for the day. Teach him how to fish and you get rid of him for the whole weekend.
Zenna Schaffer

My racehorses look remarkably healthy. That's because they don't sit up all night playing cards and drinking vodka.

Fred Winter

When a referee is in doubt, I think he is justified in deciding against the side that makes the most noise.

A. H. Almond

It's not good sportsmanship to pick up lost golf balls while they are still rolling.

Mark Twain

The only difference between me and General Custer is that I have to watch the films on Sunday.

Rick Venturi

Having small hands, I was becoming terribly self-conscious about keeping the second tennis ball in a can in the car while I served the first.

Erma Bombeck

Poker is a game of chance, but not the way I play it.

W. C. Fields

In 1876 the jockey Fred Archer blew his brains out at Newmarket. Knowing the place pretty well, I suspect he was trying to attract the attention of the staff in the Rutland Hotel.

Jeffrey Bernard

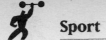

The Extraordinary Achievement Award goes to Billy Martin for having reached the age of fifty without being murdered by someone, to the amazement of all who knew him.

Murray Chase

I am the greatest golfer in the world. I just haven't played yet.

Muhammad Ali

The new West Stand casts a giant shadow over the entire pitch even on a sunny day.

Chris Jones

Pancho Gonzales was the most even-tempered man I ever knew. Always mad.

Ben Thomas

I don't like all-in wrestling – if it's all in, why wrestle?

Mae West

The bowler had the batsman in two minds. He didn't know whether to hit him for four or six.

Arthur Wood

I always know which side a putt will break; it slopes toward the part of the green my overweight caddie Herman is standing on.

Lee Trevino

Joe who did you say? Oh, Frazier. Yeah, I remember him. He's the one who leads with his face all the time.

Muhammad Ali

No, I never broke my nose playing ice hockey; but eleven other guys did.

Gordie Howe

John Barnes' problem is that he gets injured appearing on A Question of Sport.

Tommy Docherty

Tommy Smith could start a riot in a graveyard.

Bill Shankly

The most famous recipe in racing is the one for Lester Piggott's breakfast – a cough and a copy of the *Sporting Life*.

Simon Barnes

Players and spectators at all levels can enjoy sport better if they totally accept two simple rules. Rule One: The referee is always right. Rule Two: In the event of the referee being obviously wrong, Rule One applies.

Peter Corrigan

When I was a little boy I wanted to be a baseball player and join the circus. With the Yankees I've accomplished both.

Craig Nettles

It's a funny kind of month, October. For the really keen cricket fan it's when you discover that your wife left you in May.

Dennis Norden

Sport

Managing Dunfermline Athletic is a great job, except for the Saturday afternoons.

Jocky Scott

You have to be suspicious when you line up against girls with moustaches.

Maree Holland

I've reached that awkward age for any sportsman – too old physically to carry on competing at the top level, but still too mentally alert to become a selector.

Sebastian Coe

When you win the toss, bat. If you are in doubt about it, think – then bat. If you have very big doubts, consult a colleague – then bat.

W. G. Grace

My greatest strength is that I have no weaknesses.

John McEnroe

Arnold Palmer has more people watching him park the car than I do on the course.

Lee Trevino

My theory is that if you buy an ice cream cone and make it hit your mouth, you can play tennis. If you stick it on your forehead, your chances are less.

Vic Braden

I regard golf as an expensive way of playing marbles.

G. K. Chesterton

I was asked to suggest a title for my autobiography. I said
THE DEFINITIVE VOLUME ON THE FINEST
BLOODY FAST BOWLER THAT EVER DREW
BREATH.

Freddie Trueman

Mexico City was not responsible for the New York Mets
loss. My players can lose at any altitude.

Casey Stengel

God invented golf so white people would have an excuse to
get dressed up like black people.

Stanley Morgan

The spectacle of twenty-two grown men with hairy legs
chasing a bladder filled with air from one end of a field to
another is both ludicrous and infantile.

George Bernard Shaw

The only time Ray Wilkins goes forward is to toss the coin.

Tommy Docherty

In the pole vault Cassidy did twenty feet but he was
disqualified. He didn't come down.

Frank Carson

Alright everyone, line up alphabetically according to your
height.

Casey Stengel

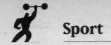

Sport

If there is a group of men doing anything with a ball in a field, another group of men will watch.

Jasmine Birtles

Trevor Brooking stings like a butterfly.

Brian Clough

If Everton were playing down at the bottom of my garden, I would draw the curtains.

Bill Shankly

When you come to a fork in the road, take it.

Yogi Berra

Never bet with a bookmaker if you see him knocking spikes in his shoes.

Jack Leach

I am prepared to offer better odds on an alien landing on earth than a Briton winning the men's singles at Wimbledon.

William Hill

A run of good luck is a sure sign of bad luck.

Walt Kelly

Half the things I said, I never said them.

Yogi Berra

God is love – but Satan is thirty and two sets to one up.

Don Geddis

Despite my best efforts and intentions, the Olympic Games still get to me. Blearily I look up and realise it's 3:30 am and I've spent four hours watching small blank-faced Eastern European girls jumping over furniture.

A. A. Gill

Seve Ballesteros is never in trouble. He's in the trees quite a lot, but that's not trouble for him – that's normal.

Ben Crenshaw

I called my dachshund "fast bowler" because he has four short legs and can swing balls both ways.

Brian Johnson

When the fight was over my opponent was all covered in blood – my blood.

Jimmy Durante

Why doesn't the fattest man in the world become a hockey goalie?

Wright Stevens

Football players, like prostitutes are in the business of ruining their bodies for the pleasure of strangers.

Merle Kessler

They should call it a swimming "ool" because the "p" is silent.

Patrick Murray

A reporter asked me what was the turning point in my match with Ben Hogan. I told him it was when Hogan showed up.

Jimmy Demaret

I got fired because of my age. I'll never make the mistake of being seventy again.

Casey Stengel

Chess is a foolish expedient for making foolish people believe that they are doing something very clever when they are only wasting their time.

George Bernard Shaw

When I was asked to write my autobiography I asked them "On what?"

Chris Eubank

The Scottish football fans' ability to smuggle drink into football matches makes Papillon look like an amateur.

Patrick Murray

I never comment on referees and I'm not going to break the habit of a lifetime for that prat.

Ron Atkinson

If you can't be an athlete at least be an athletic supporter.

Eve Arden

Men hate to lose. I once beat my husband at tennis. I asked him, "Are we going to have sex again?" He said "Yes, but not with each other."

Rita Rudner

The only interesting part of skiing is seeing someone crash. Violently.

Denis Leary

I've done for golf what Truman Capote did for Sumo wrestling.

Bob Hope

If the world were a logical place, men would ride side saddle.

Rita Mae Brown

Tony Brown is wrestling competitively at 105 pounds, a year after having both legs amputated in an accident. He is one of the bravest people I know.

Steve Komac

On one hole I'm like Arnold Palmer; at the next I'm Lilli Palmer.

Sean Connery

My mum says I used to fight my way out of the cot, but I can't remember. That was before my time.

Frank Bruno

Sport

Women's sport, especially on television, is really just an excuse to give some dirty old man a thrill as they get a chance to see a flash of frilly knicks and a couple of bobbing boobs.

Joan Burnie

Baseball has the advantage over cricket of being sooner ended.

George Bernard Shaw

Theatre and Criticism

A. E. Matthews ambled his way through the play like a charming retriever who had buried a bone and couldn't quite remember where.

Noel Coward

Drama critics are there to show gay actors what it is like to have a wife.

Hugh Leonard

Ralph Richardson is the glass eye in the forehead of English acting.

Kenneth Tynan

In this production of *Macbeth*, the prompter stole the show.

Peter Lewis

Nudity on stage? I think it's digusting. But if I were twenty-two with a great body, it would be artistic, tasteful, patriotic and a religious experience.

Shelley Winters

It was the kind of show where the girls were not auditioned – just measured.

Irene Thomas

The plays of Samuel Beckett remind me of something Sir John Betjeman might do if you filled him up with benzedrine and then forcefed him with Guinness intravenously.

Tom Davis

What should the theatre be? The theatre should be full.

Giuseppe Verdi

I would just like to mention Robert Houdin, who invented in the eighteenth century the vanishing bird cage trick and the theatre matinée – may he rot and perish. Good afternoon.

Orson Welles

On the stage David Garrick was natural, simple, affecting. It was only when he was off that he was acting.

Oliver Goldsmith

The conscientious Canadian critic is one who subscribes to the *New York Times* so that he knows at first hand what his opinions should be.

Eric Nichol

Your criticism hurt me so much, I cried all the way to the bank.

Liberace

Show me a critic without prejudices and I'll show you an arrested cretin.

George Nathan

How Henry Irving would have loved his funeral.

Ellen Terry

George Burns is old enough to be his father.

Red Buttons

As an actress, her only flair is in her nostrils.

Pauline Kael

Edward Woodward – his name sounds like someone farting in the bath.

Noel Coward

It's not easy being a comedian. Some do it by wearing funny clothes, some comedians have a funny face. Me? I have this curse of beauty.

Frankie Howerd

Critics are just eunuchs at a gang bang.

George Burns

Acting is just shouting in the evening.

Patrick Troughton

Kenneth Tynan as the First Player in *Hamlet* was quite dreadful. He would not get a chance in a village hall unless he was related to the vicar.

Beverly Baxter

Rather an unpleasant family, those Lears.

W. P. Ridge

A dramatic critic is a newspaperman whose sweetheart ran away with an actor.

Walter Winchell

Audiences are just coughing bastards.

Donald Wolfit

I'm in bed with Burt Reynolds most of the time in the play.
Oh, I know it's dirty work, but somebody has to do it.

Carol Burnett

The number of arrests following the circulation of Alec
Guinness's description would break all records.

Kenneth Tynan

It was easy enough to make Al Jolson happy at home. You
just had to cheer him for breakfast, applaud wildly for lunch
and give him a standing ovation for dinner.

George Burns

I have no objections to long tedious plays. I always feel fresh
when I wake up at the end.

John B. Keane

They sent Oscar Wilde, that poor man, to Reading Gaol for
doing what all other actors today get knighted for.

Wilfrid Hyde White

Mister Robinson is suffering from delusions of adequacy.

Walter Kerr

I suppose I could make changes in my play but who am I to
tamper with a masterpiece?

Oscar Wilde

Last time I performed my name was so low on the programme I was getting orders for the printing.

Frank Carson

William Green hasn't got a head. His neck just grew up and haired over.

John L. Lewis

Mr. Lore's idea of playing a he-man was to extend his chest three inches and then follow it slowly across the stage.

Heywood Broun

Actors like Shakespeare because they can gum on a lot of crepe hair, bellow almost anything that comes into their heads and then have their Lear taken seriously by the critics.

J. B. Priestley

If this play lasts overnight it should not only be considered a long run but a revival as well.

Alexander Woollcott

I think that first nights should come near the end of a play's run – as indeed they often do.

Peter Ustinov

She knows when she should come on and she knows when she should go off – it's the bit in between that foxes her.

Hugh Hunt

Theatre and Criticism

Lady Longford's play about homosexuality marks the beginning of the Sodom and Begorra school.

Lionel Hale

I regret to say that the patrons of the gallery, being admitted at half the usual West End price, devote the saving to the purchase of sausages to throw at the critics. I appeal to the gentleman or lady who successfully aimed one at me to throw a cabbage next time, as I am a vegetarian and sausages are wasted on me.

George Bernard Shaw

Mary Martin is OK if you like talent.

Ethel Merman

I should like you to convey when you are acting it that the man you portray has a brother in Shropshire who drinks port.

J. M. Barrie

What, an actor asking for a salary when blackberries are ripe?

John S. Potter

A woman complimenting me on my act one night told me she hadn't laughed so much since her husband died.

Victor Borge

It is a great help for a man to be in love with himself. For an actor it is absolutely essential.

Robert Morley

Dramatic criticism is venom from contented snakes.

Percy Hammond

How do you become a comic? First of all you must get your potential spotted. You can always get it off later with turps.

Ken Dodd

Among the select group of plays written for husband and wife teams in the coronation years, *The Sleeping Prince*, starring Laurence Olivier and Vivien Leigh, ranks very high.

Kenneth Tynan

Del Prete has as much charm as a broomstick with a smile painted on it.

John Simon

Michael Caine can out-act any, well nearly any, telephone kiosk you care to mention.

Hugh Leonard

As for Sheperd's dancing, the best to be said is that it may not be recognisable as such: When this horsey ex-model starts prancing around, she tends to look as if she's fighting off a chronic case of trots.

Frank Rich

Steve Martin has basically one joke and he's it.

Dave Felton

Bob Newhart can bite the hand that feeds him and make it feel like a manicure.

Gilbert Millstein

Mary Poppins is unsupercalifragilisticexpialidocious.

Gilbert Adair

Theatre and Criticism

Show me a great actor and I'll show you a lousy husband.
Show me a great actress and you've seen the devil.

W. C. Fields

One of my plays enjoyed a continuous run of one successive
night.

Brander Matthews

They smiled at the joke, not because they were amused, but
because they wished to show respect for old age.

Strickland Gillilan

Every playwright should try acting, just as every judge
should spend some weeks in jail, to find out what he is
handing out to others.

E. M. Remarque

Often as he sneered at Plato, Aristotle never called him a
playwright.

Max Beerbohm

Don't give complimentary tickets. If your friends won't pay
to see you, who will?

Oswald Stoll

The only talent Doris Day possesses is that of being
absolutely sanitary; her personality untouched by human
emotions, her brow unclouded by human thought, her form
unsmudged by the slightest evidence of femininity.

John Simon

Barbra Streisand looks like a cross between an aardvark and an albino rat surmounted by a platinum coated horse bun.

John Simon

Don't pay any attention to critics – don't even ignore them.

Sam Goldwyn

Derek Jacobi had a brilliant performance in One Claudius.

Terry Wogan

Mae West was a plumber's idea of Cleopatra.

W. C. Fields

I do not hate the critics. I have nothing but compassion for them. How can I hate the crippled, the mentally deficient and the dead?

Albert Finney

Maureen O'Hara looks as if butter wouldn't melt in her mouth – or anywhere else either.

Elsa Lancaster

Miscellaneous

National Service did the country a lot of good, but it darned near killed the army.

Richard Hull

I am so unlucky that I run into accidents that started out to happen to someone else.

Don Marquis

Social work is a band-aid on the festering wounds of society.

Alexander Chase

It is difficult to see why lace should be so expensive; it is mostly holes.

Mary W. Little

The cat, having sat upon a hot stove lid, will not sit upon a hot stove lid again. Nor upon a cold lid.

Mark Twain

That rabbit's foot you carry for good luck wasn't very lucky for the rabbit, was it?

R. E. Shay

If a thing is worth doing, it's worth doing badly.

G. K. Chesterton

A moose is an animal with horns on the front of his head and a hunting lodge wall on the back of it.

Groucho Marx

Miscellaneous

Many a man has decided to stay alive, not because of the will to live, but because of the determination not to give assorted surviving bastards the satisfaction of his death.

Brendan Francis

If God had meant us to travel tourist class, he would have made us narrower.

Martha Zimmerman

The trouble with morning is that it always comes at such an ungodly hour.

Dominic Cleary

Nothing is so useless as a general maxim.

Thomas B. Macaulay

If God had meant us to walk around naked, he would never have invented the wicker chair.

Erma Bombeck

They claim to be he-men, but the hair from their combined chests wouldn't have made a wig for a grape.

Robert Benchley

British Rail porters are trained at the Pol Pot school of charm, while guards are either frustrated broadcasters, ceaselessly blaring out incomprehensible messages or Trappist monks who have taken a holy vow forbidding any form of communication whatsoever.

Victor Lewis-Smith

The trouble with letting it all hang out is the difficulty of stuffing it all back in again.

Eric Wright

He was dead alright. He had been shot, poisoned, stabbed and strangled. Either someone had really had it in for him or four people had killed him. Or else it was the cleverest suicide I'd ever seen.

Richard Prather

There are just two rules for success: 1. Never tell all you know.

Roger H. Lincoln

I love flying. I've been to almost as many places as my luggage.

Bob Hope

Corey Pavin is a little on the slight side. When he goes through the turnstile, nothing happens.

Lee Trevino

After things have gone from bad to worse, the cycle will repeat itself.

Bob Murphy

I have never understood why, when I was born, I was the one who wound up with the stretchmarks.

Linda Agran

A lot of horses get distracted – it's just human nature.

Nick Zito

A rainbow is not an optical illusion – it just looks like one.

Phil White

The more buttons done up on someone's shirt, the higher their IQ.

Curtis Cloaninger

When I rescued their cat, the ladies gave me a standing ovulation.

Willie Bermingham

The quickest way to make a red light turn green is to try to find something in the glove compartment.

Gary Doney

I hope that when insects take over the world, they will remember with gratitude how we took them along on all our picnics.

Bill Vaughan

Book returns are gone today and here tomorrow.

Alfred Knopf

Eighty per cent of pollution is caused by plants and trees.

Ronald Reagan

During the battle, I was right where the bullets were the thickest – underneath the ammunition truck.

Lou Costello

I have been accused of every death except the casualty list of World War I.

Al Capone

Magna Carta – did she die in vain?

Tony Hancock

The Magna Carta ensured that no man could be hanged twice for the same offence.

George Coote

I haven't been to sleep for over a year. That's why I go to bed early. One needs more rest if one doesn't sleep.

Evelyn Waugh

There comes a time in every man's life when he must make way for an older man.

Reginald Maudling

It was one of those perfect summer days – the sun was shining, a breeze was blowing, the birds were singing and the lawnmower was broken.

James Dent

I was stopped once for doing 53 in a 35 mile zone. I told the police I had dyslexia.

Steve McFarlin

When I appeared before the draft board examiner during World War II, he asked me if I thought I could kill. "I don't know about strangers," I replied, "but friends, certainly."

Oscar Levant

You can make up a quarrel, but it will always show where it was patched.

E. W Howe

Crime pays. You get to travel a lot and the hours are good.

Woody Allen

I have a prodigious quantity of mind. It takes me as much as a week, sometimes, to make it up.

Mark Twain

The person who makes a bad thirty-minute speech to two hundred people wastes only half an hour of his own time. But he wastes one hundred hours of the audience's time – more than four days, which should be a hanging offence.

Jenkin L. Jones

Miscellaneous

We have to believe in free will – we have no choice.

Isaac Singer

I have yet to see any problem, however complicated, which when you looked at it in the right way, did not become still more complicated.

Poul Anderson

You've got to be very careful if you don't know where you're going because you might not get there.

Yogi Berra

I'm so fat that when I have my shoes cleaned, I have to take the shoeshine boy's word for it.

Stubby Kaye

Rule one of the book of war is: Don't march on Moscow.

Bernard Montgomery

If you're not part of the solution, you're part of the precipitate.

Steven Wright

There are two kinds of statistics, the kind you look up and the kind you make up.

Rex Stout

I told him to take a picture of his testicles so he'd have something to remember them by if he ever hit me again.

Bobby Knight

Miscellaneous

The man who walks alone will soon be trailed by the FBI.

Wright Morris

Get your rooms full of good air and then shut up the windows and keep it. It will keep for years. Anyway, don't keep using your lungs all the time. Let them rest.

Stephen Leacock

Ready, fire, aim.

Spike Milligan

A job is death without the dignity.

Brendan Behan

Digging the garden might seem less fun than going fishing, but not to a worm.

Clyde Abel

When going abroad, get yourself a decent hamper from Fortnum and Mason's and keep away from the native women.

Edward Evans

The last time I saw him, he was walking down Lovers' Lane, holding his own hand.

Fred Allen

I always travel third class because there is no fourth class.

George Santayana

Right now, I'm having amnesia and déjà vu at the same time. I think I've forgotten this before.

Steven Wright

In certain parts of the world people still pray in the streets. In this country, they're called pedestrians.

Gloria Pitzner

P. J. O'Rourke has a perfect New Right name – hard Irish, with a hint of pyjamas.

A. A. Gill

Paul Johnson is a red-haired, red-faced man of sixty-five, seemingly in transit between Dr. Jekyll and Mr. Hyde.

Peter McKay

You should avoid clichés like the plague.

Samuel Goldwyn

Jack "Legs" Diamond could tie both his shoes at once.

William Kennedy

I phoned my local cab firm and said: "Can you please send me a big fat racist bastard with a personal hygiene problem some time before I have my menopause?"

Jo Brand

If skirts get any shorter, I'm gonna have to get my legs fixed. They don't go all the way up.

Phyllis Diller

Hanging is too good for a man who makes puns; he should be drawn and quoted.

Fred Allen

I like to skate on the other side of the ice.

Steven Wright

Mary Baker Eddy had much in common with Hitler, only no moustache.

Noel Coward

People often say to me "Emo"; you see, they're afraid I'll reproduce.

Emo Philips

I joined Liars Anonymous, but I had a lot of trouble finding them because they put the wrong address on all their ads.

J. J. Waugh

How long does it take me to have my hair done? I don't know – I'm never there.

Dolly Parton

My luck is so bad that if I bought ducks the bastards would drown.

Patrick Murray

Be optimistic, be positive. I said I can, I do and I did. I got three months for it.

Ken Dodd

You should never put your best trousers on when you go out
to fight for freedom and truth.

Henrik Ibsen

Hush, hush, nobody cares; Christopher Robin has fallen
downstairs.

J. B. Morton

A soiled baby with a neglected nose cannot be
conscientiously regarded as a thing of beauty.

Mark Twain

Never in the history of fashion has so little material been
raised so high to reveal so much that needs to be covered so
badly.

Cecil Beaton

A diary is the daily record of that part of one's life which he
can relate to himself without blushing.

Ambrose Bierce

I have the very highest opinion of scandal. It is founded on
the most sacred of things – that is, Truth, and it is built up by
the most beautiful of things – that is, Imagination.

William Mallock

You ought to take the bull by the teeth.

Samuel Goldwyn

Heywood Broun is a one-man slum.

Alexander Woollcott

To give you an idea of how fast we travelled – we left with two rabbits and when we arrived we still had only two.

Bob Hope

The world contrived to get on before I was born (I don't quite know how) and I dare say it will make some sort of lame shift after I am dead.

George Bernard Shaw

He led his regiment from behind – he found it less exciting.

William S. Gilbert

How is it that the first piece of luggage on the airport carousel never belongs to anyone?

George Roberts

What the world needs is more geniuses with humility; there are so few of us left.

Oscar Levant

Dwn wth vwls.

Ruth Ollins

No matter what side of the argument you're on, you always find some people on your side that you wish were on the other side.

Jascha Heifetz

Basically the word mankind is made up of two separate words, mank and ind. What do these words mean? Nobody knows and that is why mankind is a mystery.

Jack Handey

I am a topless dancer, but I see myself as a humanitarian, whatever that means.

Carol Doda

When I found the skull in the woods, the first thing I did was call the police, but then I got curious about it. I picked it up and started wondering about who this person was and why he had deer horns.

Jack Handey

It's spreading like wildflowers.

Samuel Goldwyn

Homelessness is homelessness no matter where you live.

Glenda Jackson

Coffee just isn't my cup of tea.

Samuel Goldwyn

I got a new shadow. I had to get rid of the other one. It wasn't doing what I was doing.

Steven Wright

I have a very rare photograph — it's a picture of Houdini trying to rescue his keys out of a locked car.

Steven Wright

It is rare to find learned men who are clean, do not stink and have a sense of humour.

Montesquieu

If I could drop dead right now, I'd be the happiest man alive.

Samuel Goldwyn

My latest girlfriend is a bilingual illiterate – she can't read in two different languages.

Steven Wright

When in doubt, use brute force.

Ken Thompson

Thieves respect property. They merely wish the property to become their property that they may more perfectly respect it.

G. K. Chesterton

It is worse than immoral – it is a mistake.

Dean Acheson

Listen, everybody is entitled to my opinion.

Madonna

I can picture in my mind a world without war, a world without hate. And I can picture us attacking that world, because they would never expect it.

Jack Handey

I could dance with you until the cows come home. On second thoughts I'd rather dance with the cows until you come home.

Groucho Marx

Under a forehead roughly comparable to that of Javanese and Piltdown man, there are visible S. J. Perelman's pair of eyes lit up alternately by greed and concupiscence.

S. J. Perelman

I am dying. What an irreparable loss to the world.

Auguste Comte

As the light changed from red to green to amber and back to red again, I sat there thinking about life. Was it nothing more than a lot of honking and yelling? Sometimes it seemed that way.

Jack Handey

It's a funny old world. It's a lucky man who gets out of it alive.

W. C. Fields

I learned long ago that racehorses, women and fish are smarter than I am.

Raymond Myers

I went to a museum that had all the heads and arms from the statues that are in all the other museums.

Steven Wright

In painting a ceiling a good rule of thumb is that there should be at least as much paint on the ceiling as on your hair.

P. J. O'Rourke

The intelligence of the planet is constant and the population is growing.

Arthur C. Clarke

The modern definition of a racist is someone who wins an argument with a liberal.

Peter Brimelow

An optimist is a guy that never had much experience.

Don Marquis

We have more to fear from the bungling of the incompetent than from the machinations of the wicked.

R. L. Meller

A redneck died and left his entire fortune to his beloved wife. She couldn't touch it until she was fourteen.

Jeff Foxworthy

Once we brought an invisible horse on stage but nobody could see it because it was parked behind the invisible steam-roller.

Vic Reeves

No matter which side of the toe of a sock the hole is in, you will always put the sock on so that your big toe protrudes through the hole.

Tom Eddins

The extra holes in notebook paper are there in the hopes that one day mankind will perfect a five-ring binder.

David Chapman

I ran three miles today and finally I said, "Lady, take your purse."

Emo Philips

Sufficiently advanced political correctness is indistinguishable from sarcasm.

Eric Naggum

An expert is a man who never makes small mistakes.

Tom Phipps

Tell me your phobias and I'll tell you what you are afraid of.

Robert Benchley

The duel is one of the most dangerous institutions; since it is always fought in the open at daybreak, the combatants are sure to catch cold.

Mark Twain

Tell a man that there are 500 billion stars in the universe and he will believe you. Tell him a fence has just been painted and he has to touch it to find out that it has been.

Herb Cohen

Applause before a speaker begins is an act of faith. Applause during the speech is an act of hope. Applause after he has concluded is an act of charity.

Fulton J. Sheen

If you've heard this before, don't stop me because I'd like to hear it again.

Groucho Marx

Handsome? He looked like a dog's bum with a hat on.

Spike Milligan

A petition is a list of people who didn't have the courage to say no.

Evan Esar

Moanday, tearday, wailsday, thumpsday, frightday, shatterday, shunday.

James Joyce

Patience is a minor form of despair, disguised as a virtue.

Ambrose Bierce

In the army I knew more about retreating than the man who invented retreating.

Mark Twain

It's amazing how long it takes to complete something you're not working on.

R. D. Clyde

Behrman – forgotten but not gone.

George S. Kaufman

I've always been a bit more maturer than what I am.

Samantha Fox

We'll burn that bridge when we come to it.

Matt Goukas

The Paris EuroDisney makes the British theme parks look like Mickey Mouse affairs.

Neil Walker

Like a midget at a urinal I have to stay on my toes.

Leslie Nielsen

Have you heard about the oyster who went to a disco and pulled a mussel?

Billy Connolly

When you hear a man speak of his love for his country, it is a sign he expects to be paid for it.

H. L. Mencken

When Solomon said there was a time and a place for everything, he had not encountered the problem of parking an automobile.

Bob Edwards

I've got nothing to say. And I'll say it only once.

Floyd Smith

The trouble with her is that she lacks the power of conversation but not the power of speech.

George Bernard Shaw

Under my flabby exterior lies an enormous lack of character.

Oscar Levant

The best years are the forties; after fifty a man begins to deteriorate, but in the forties he is at the maximum of his villainy.

H. L. Mencken

Index

Index

Index

Index

Index

Index

Index

Index

Index

Index

Index

Index

Index

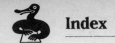 **Index**